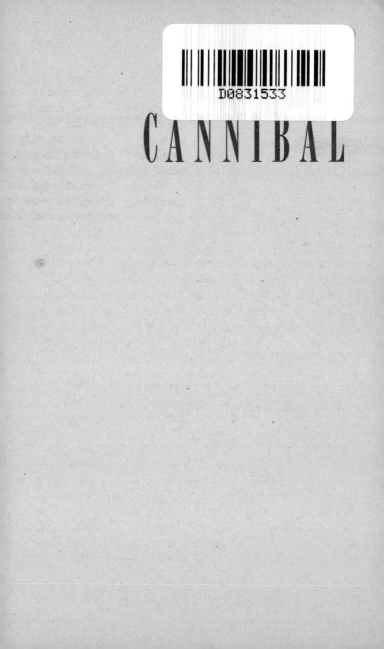

CANNIBAL

CANNIBAL

The True Story
Behind the
Maneater
of Rotenburg

LOIS JONES

BERKLEY BOOKS, NEW YORK

THE BERKLEY PUBLISHING GROUP
Published by the Penguin Group
Penguin Group (USA) Inc.
375 Hudson Street, New York, New York 10014, USA
Penguin Group (Canada), 10 Alcorn Avenue, Toronto, Ontario M4V 3B2, Canada
(a division of Pearson Penguin Canada Inc.)
Penguin Books Ltd., 80 Strand, London WC2R 0RL, England
Penguin Group Ireland, 25 St. Stephen's Green, Dublin 2, Ireland (a division of Penguin Books Ltd.)
Penguin Group (Australia), 250 Camberwell Road, Camberwell, Victoria 3124, Australia
(a division of Pearson Australia Group Pty. Ltd.)
Penguin Books India Pvt. Ltd., 11 Community Centre, Panchsheel Park, New Delhi—110 017, India
Penguin Group (NZ), cnr Airborne and Rosedale Roads, Albany, Auckland 1310, New Zealand
(a division of Pearson New Zealand Ltd.)
Penguin Books (South Africa) (Pty.) Ltd., 24 Sturdee Avenue, Rosebank, Johannesburg 2196,
South Africa

Penguin Books Ltd., Registered Offices: 80 Strand, London WC2R 0RL, England

CANNIBAL

A Berkley Book / published by arrangement with the author

PRINTING HISTORY
Berkley mass-market edition / January 2005

Copyright © 2005 by Lois Jones
Cover photo © AP/Wide World Photos
Book design by Stacy Irwin

ISBN: 0-425-20066-3

BERKLEY®
Berkley Books are published by The Berkley Publishing Group,
a division of Penguin Group (USA) Inc.,
375 Hudson Street, New York, New York 10014.
BERKLEY is a registered trademark of Penguin Group (USA) Inc.
The "B" design is a trademark belonging to Penguin Group (USA) Inc.

PRINTED IN THE UNITED STATES OF AMERICA

10 9 8 7 6 5 4 3 2 1

This book
is dedicated
to Barnaby
and my family
for their love,
support
and belief
in me.

ACKNOWLEDGMENTS

I would like to thank many for their help in creating this book.

For their love and support, I thank Barnaby, my parents and Howard and Gayle. A special thanks goes to Clive for his eternal encouragement and daily cheer.

I am also grateful to Flavia, Rachel, Lynne and Bartlin for their sound advice.

For her careful attention to the manuscript, professionalism and positive words, I thank my editor, Allison McCabe.

I am also grateful for the assistance provided by Frank Thonicke, HNA; Channel Four and Stern.

All the names in this book are real. The events in this book are real, or as close to real as humanly possible. The story that follows is based on hours of research, interviews and first-person accounts of the participants.

Preparations
for
Dinner

The sun shone down on the half timbered farmhouse, nestling in the rolling hills of central Germany. It was a Friday in March 2001, just before Easter.

The birds were singing, welcoming in the spring. The picturesque hamlet was otherwise silent, apart from the sound of a tractor trundling through the nearby fields. Occasionally a car drove past the farmhouse and down the lane that led through Wüstefeld, a secluded area of Rotenburg an der Fulda in the German state of Hesse. Visitors were few to this country idyll on the edge of nowhere, and the thirty or so inhabitants liked it that way. Families from the six houses in the settlement knew one another's business, or so they liked to think.

The Brothers Grimm wrote many of their fairy tales in nearby Kassel, populating the thickly forested countryside around the farmhouse with dwarfs, goblins and witches. There is a museum in Kassel celebrating their work. Kassel's highlights also include the Museum of Death, with its permanent collection of headstones, hearses and death-depicting sculptures.

Armin Meiwes, whose family had first bought the rambling, thirty-room farmhouse on a rental basis back in 1965, loved the Brothers Grimm's fantastical tales. His favorite childhood story had always been "Hansel and Gretel," particularly the passage in which the storybook witch "fattens up little Hansel" in the hope of cooking him and eating him. As a child he used to act out the scene time and again, playing the role of the witch and delighting in the idea of roasting and devouring Hansel.

Armin's family spent most of their holidays at this farmhouse, with its stables and large garden, surrounded by meadows. Young Armin would look after his beloved pony, Polly, and take his dog, an Alsation, for walks. He would play with his neighbor, Manfred Stück, whose grandfather eventually sold the house to them. The farm wasn't popular with other local children, who called it the "haunted house" because of its dark interior and musty smell. When he was sixteen, Armin moved to the sprawling estate full-time and lived there with his mother.

The farmhouse today is an edifice of dust-filled corners and rooms thick with cobwebs. Armin's mother had furnished it according to her taste, with floral carpets and antique furniture from the Biedermeier era, a period in mid-nineteenth century Germany known for its solidity and conventionality. And after she died, Armin never changed it. Visitors to the house feel as if they have been transported back a century or two.

Outside, a child's swing set sits forlornly in a tangle of high grass and rots away alongside a heap of tires, broken lawnmowers and six old cars Armin had always intended to restore but had never gotten around to. He lived mainly on the ground floor of the house. Computer screens and hardware littered the room where he spent most of his evenings, surfing the Internet for hours. Most of the other rooms were guest rooms. The beds were always made up in case anyone came to stay. But nobody ever did. Now that his mother was dead, Armin lived alone with his memories, computers and a Persian cat, Cleo, for company.

Today, though, Armin, a forty-year old computer expert, was expecting company.

Bernd Juergen Brandes, a computer engineer, was coming for dinner.

Armin had stocked up on bottles of his favorite South African red Merlot and bought lots of brussels sprouts, porcini and potatoes. He liked olive oil and garlic, so he made sure he had plenty in stock. He licked his lips at the thought of the meal ahead. Succulent, tender flesh like he had never tasted before.

His stomach growled in hungry anticipation.

Armin had never met Bernd, but they already felt close. Indeed, the two seemed like soul mates. They had become acquainted over a gay Internet chat line, and had exchanged a stream of e-mails over the last few months, revealing to each other their innermost sexual thoughts and festering desires. They both harbored violent sexual fantasies. The two spent hours online feeding their need for pornographic images of torture, abuse and sadomasochism. Pain was their pleasure. Leather, rubber and erotic scenes of domination and submission were a big turn-on. But these two weren't hoping to indulge in S&M role-plays. What made these new friends so unusual was their mutual obsession with cannibalism and the way their sexual preferences in this area gelled.

One wanted to kill and eat someone, and the other wanted to be killed and eaten.

And they advertised the fact.

In late 2000, in one of his favorite Internet chat rooms

catering to cannibals, Armin posted an ad: "Seeking well-built man, 18–30 years old, for slaughter." A few months later, Bernd replied: "I offer myself to you and will let you dine from my live body. Not butchery, dining!"

The pair set up a bizarre contract designed to realize each other's lifelong desires. Armin, fascinated by cannibalism since an early age, was to kill, dismember and devour his victim to satisfy his longing for human flesh. Bernd wanted to be castrated, killed and eaten to annihilate any last traces of himself on earth. He had wanted to be slaughtered and eaten since he was a young boy.

The Internet had made it possible for this odd couple to find each other.

Without it, they probably would have kept their fantasies hidden and never would have met.

Armin smiled to himself and felt a tender feeling inside as he thought of Bernd's last e-mail to him. "There's absolutely no way back for me, only forwards, through your teeth," Bernd had written.

For Armin, there could be no sweeter love letter.

Armin's Childhood

Waltraud Meiwes was almost forty years old when she brought Armin, her third and last son, into the world. It was 1961. The child's face was set in the same cast as his mother's, with identical deep-set eyes, thin lips and a long, sharp nose. Armin wasn't a handsome child, but his open face was pleasant.

He spent his early childhood in Essen-Holsterhausen, in the Ruhr industrial area of Western Germany. He lived there with his mother, his two half-brothers from his mother's first marriage, and his father, a policeman. When he was eight years old, the men disappeared out of his life. First his younger half-brother, Ingbert, went off to live with his biological father in Berlin. Then his father, Dieter, separated from his mother. Armin's mother (who was nineteen years older than his father) and Dieter had been at each other's throat, and Dieter could no longer take the stress of their daily domestic disputes. "There's nothing left to save in our marriage anymore," he calmly stated to his wife one evening during one of their confrontations. "We fight every day. I can't take it anymore."

"You're having an affair," Waltraud screamed. "Who is she? I'm going to kill her."

Waltraud launched into another hysterical outpouring of jealous accusations. Dieter shrugged it off; it didn't touch him anymore, he just wanted out. *At least Armin should turn out okay despite this mess,* Dieter thought to himself. *He's such a calm, well-behaved little boy.* He gazed down at his son, who was quietly amusing himself building model houses. He looked so young and innocent. Dieter had no inkling of his son's Hansel and Gretel obsession, or of the darker fantasies breeding inside him.

After the separation, Dieter limited contact with his son to a regular paycheck for child maintenance and strained visits every year or two. Armin felt lonely and missed his dad and his half-brother. He even missed the squabbles with his brother, and the yells from his parents screaming at each other. At least there had been some noise then; the house was a lot quieter now. Then his favorite half-brother, Wolfgang, the eldest one, moved to Berlin to be with his father, and Armin was left alone in his mother's custody.

With his eldest half-brother gone too, Armin, age six, had just his mother for company—an embittered, middle-aged woman who felt she had been dragged down by her second broken marriage. She was a proud woman who had come from a well-off family and expected to do well for herself. Her youngest son was the last man in her life, and she would chain him to her side.

Waltraud hardened after her second marriage collapsed and her family fell apart. She never smiled anymore; instead she wore a permanent expression of disapproval, and nothing seemed strong enough to break through her armor of sourness. She felt a powerful hate toward the two ex-husbands who had failed her, abandoned her and destroyed her dreams. She spent her days remorselessly bullying little Armin, letting her youngest son and everyone who came near her taste her bitterness.

She wrote up her family history in notebooks and had it printed. She wrote about the slaughter of her forefathers in the Napoleonic wars and the First World War. She didn't waste a word writing about her sons and ex-husbands. They didn't exist for her now; in her new universe, she was the only one who counted.

Armin toed the line at school as well as at home.

He did well at his school subjects, particularly math. He was bright and conscientious, always doing his homework. Sometimes he got into fights, but he never landed himself or others in big trouble, or did anything to cause himself to be hauled in front of the school principal. However, he never seemed able to make friends.

A shy, inhibited boy, he avoided joining in schoolyard games and rarely joked with his classmates. He didn't know any of the latest toys or have any cool gadgets like the other boys. So why would anyone want to be his friend? Besides it was far easier to laugh at him. He was the "kooky one," the "mama's boy," the "oddball." His clothes provided the biggest source of amusement. His mother exposed him to unrelenting mockery from his classmates by forcing him to wear a traditional white shirt with Bavarian-style lederhosen to school. It was the beginning of the 1970s; all the other boys in his class were wearing jeans to school. He just didn't fit in.

At lunchtime, when classes finished, Armin would say goodbye to his classmates. He couldn't play, he had to go home and help his mother. Armin's work wasn't over after school finished for the day—he still had to clean the windows, wash up and take the trash out. He had his orders to follow. His mother called him "Minchen," an affectionate form of Armin that also means "servant" in old German. She was the master and he was the servant in this household.

Once or twice school friends knocked on the door and asked the shy, little boy out to play. But they were told curtly by his mother that "Minchen had been naughty and was grounded." And Minchen kept quiet and smiled. He always did what he was told. He had long ago given up fighting against his mother's humiliating orders, rants and raves. She was the boss and it was pointless protesting. "Armin, what games do you want to play?" teachers would ask him during play-break. Armin didn't know—he wanted to please everyone, and do whatever they wanted him to do. Dominated by his mother, he was never given the chance to develop his own identity.

Isolated, Armin's only example of happy family life were stolen minutes he spent with his neighbors, watching animals being slaughtered on the local farm. Pigs, ducks, hens, geese, a deer, a wild hog—all were killed to be eaten. Slaughter became an everyday event for him, one he associated with love.

At night, he dreamt of having a proper family of his own. He wanted someone to play with, to look after him, to give him a hug. As there was no one around to do that, he had to invent someone. Alone in bed, Armin started talking to a new imaginary friend. Frank, or Franky, was his name, just like the nice boy at school whom everybody liked and looked up to. Just like the little boy Armin wanted to be. Franky soon became Armin's confidant and his best friend. Armin told him all his secrets, safe in the knowledge that Franky liked him and understood him. "I miss my dad and my brother," he would whisper to Franky alone in his room at night. "We used to share this room before you lived here, Franky."

"Mother isn't happy with me again," he'd say. "I forgot to take out the trash." Or sometimes Armin told Franky how angry he was. "I don't like the new boy at school. He made fun of me again today."

And Franky told Armin how much he loved him.

Between the ages of eight and twelve, Armin developed feelings and fantasies he knew he should only share with Franky. He knew Franky would understand, though Franky was no longer the only character in Armin's dream world. Nowadays it was inhabited by other little boys and girls whom he could eat. Armin's mind soared away during the long nights to a world where he could kill, cut to pieces and devour someone. His classmates were his mealtime choices. His favorite TV program was *Flipper*, not because he liked watching the adventures with the friendly dolphin who starred in the series, but because Armin wanted to eat the dolphin's owner, Sandy. The young TV star was Armin's ideal: young, fit and blond. Just the kind of perfect, popular and successful boy he wanted to internalize. He could then take on his characteristics and become just like him—or so he believed.

"He'll never leave me if I eat Sandy or a boy from school," Armin said to Franky. "I could have someone who is always with me. I can feel safe and secure and I won't be lonely anymore. I'll have someone to be part of me."

And Franky agreed with Armin. It would be a good thing to do. Armin should have "someone to be part of him." Someone who wouldn't leave him, betray him or ever be unfaithful. Someone to be with him forever and ever.

•   •   •

Armin wanted to stop feeling lonely. He wanted to fill the painful emptiness that had flooded his insides since his father and brothers left. He wanted to eat someone to keep with him.

Whenever he had the chance, Armin watched the most gruesome horror movies he could find. His eyes hungrily consumed the scenes where bodies were ripped apart and organs were exposed. The blood and gore provided fodder for his daydreams of slaughter. This was his internal world where nobody could interfere or tell him what to do. He was boss of his private universe of death and destruction. Thoughts of eating someone fed on the introverted boy's inner turmoil and spread their roots. The fantasies had taken seed and were growing quickly, encircling their tendrils around the boy's imagination.

By the time he reached puberty at twelve, the idea of eating another boy had started to arouse Armin sexually. The idea of cutting open chests, ripping out hearts, livers and lungs and eating them while they were still warm aroused him. While other boys of his age cast hungry, curious glances in the direction of their friends' sisters and at the young girls playing sports on the game fields at school, Armin's sexual fantasies were taking more of a perverse turn. When he was younger, thoughts of cannibalism simply made him feel good inside. Now his fantasies were accompanied by a rush of overpowering hormones that he found more and more difficult to suppress.

Armin was filled with longing as he gazed at the bare chests of his male schoolmates when they got changed for games. What would their nipples taste like? His eyes lingered on the policemen in their uniforms walking past, and on their taut thighs, fit for tearing apart with his teeth. Girls didn't interest him that much. Sure, their flesh would be tender and sweet, Armin thought, but it wasn't girls he wanted in his life. Besides the world needed women for reproduction. To make more children. To make the sort of family he'd always wanted but never had.

Girls were too valuable to kill.

3

Armin's
Dominant
Mother

Armin and his mother left Essen to move into the Rotenburg farmhouse when he was sixteen. There was a good high school nearby for Armin to finish his education.

It hadn't been a big wrench for them to leave Essen. They didn't have many friends or any family to miss, and Armin was glad to move permanently into the old farmhouse. There he could withdraw into dark, abandoned rooms where nobody could disturb him. It was easier for his fantasies of corpses and their flesh to take shape in the seventeenth-century house; easier to imagine he could eat someone to be at "one with him."

Waltraud, meanwhile, reveled in the idea of finally living full-time on "her estate." She had always wanted a majestic home, with planted grounds and a driveway; the thirty or so furnished rooms (most of which were never used) of the rather dilapidated farmhouse suited her ideas of grandeur. Once they moved in permanently, the divorcée sat in the house with a superior air, but her bank balance contradicted her aspirations. She didn't work, and money was tight. She had managed to secure some from her divorcée after fighting in court; in addition to that sum, there was the rent that trickled in each month from her property in Essen. There was nothing more.

Waltraud labeled each of the farmhouse rooms with a poetic name. She called her bedroom *Sonnenglanz* or "Sunlight." Her dressing room was christened *Frühtau* or "Morning dew." Upstairs in the twenty-five-square-meter attic, she built a model railway with grandiose estates, castles and farms. The attic was named "Country View." On the door of Armin's bedroom, she posted a floral-decorated sign that read *"Kinderzimmer"* or "Child's room." Even at sixteen years of age, Armin was still a child to Waltraud and she treated him like one, making his decisions and answering for him before he had a chance to speak. Her teenage son never removed this sign.

As he had on childhood vacations spent on the farm, Armin again spent time looking after and riding his pony, Polly, and taking his Alsation for walks. He rarely met up with teenage boys his own age, who spent their afternoons listening to music or comparing notes about favorite pop stars and actresses, and the girls they had crushes on at school. Only one idol was allowed in Armin's household, and that was his mother. At weekends, the two went for walks along the lane by the farmhouse, pulled along in an old cart by the pony. Armin's bourgeois mother cast haughty glances and relayed her strict principles of living, ones that were born in the 1920s or 1930s. Armin listened obediently to what she had to say and lived according to her out-of-date rules. Back at the house, he had his daily chores. "Minchen, clean the windows," she ordered. "Minchen, make the beds," she said. "Then you can polish the silverware."

There was always plenty to clean in the rambling house.

But Waltraud wasn't content being an authoritarian only in her home.

She wanted to extend her control beyond the walls of the house, and this desire was often demonstrated when the village of Wüstefeld had a party. The villagers held regular barbecues as well as Christmas and New Year parties at one another's house. They always invited Armin and his mother along, even though the Meiweses never reciprocated. "They're a bit odd but you can't leave them out, not in a small place like this," the neighbors said to each other.

Waltraud didn't enjoy one particular party.

At 10 P.M. she stood in the middle of the barn where the gathering was being held and screamed, "This music's too loud. You have to stop the party now. It's late enough. I hate loud music. Stop it now."

Her neighbors stared. "What's her problem?" muttered one of the local wives, feeling like a scolded child. "We're only having a bit of fun."

Armin was sent home to bed; he always had to be home punctually by 10 P.M. The neighbors felt sorry for him and wondered why he didn't go out and spend time with boys his own age or chase girls.

They never suspected he had homosexual tendencies.

They had no idea of his darker cannibalistic desires.

At another village party, Karl-Friedrich Schnaar, who lived with his family about a hundred meters behind the Meiweses' house and kept approximately six thousand hens and a bakery, watched Waltraud bully her sixteen-year-old son. "Armin, don't hold your cutlery like that," she chided. "Make sure you're holding your knife and fork with your fingers in the correct position. You naughty boy." Karl-Friedrich intervened to spare Armin. "Frau Meiwes, would you like to come and join me in a glass of wine?" he asked. "I'm sure Armin is behaving himself."

It was a rare reprieve; Armin rarely escaped from Waltraud's side, or from her harsh words.

He was, however, allowed to attend the next village party without his mother.

At this gathering, he sat down at a table with a group of twelve-year-old boys. With his hands folded neatly in his lap, he grinned inanely as he listened to their jokes. "Don't be such a drip, Armin," said Manfred, his neighbor's son. "Why are you sitting there with all the *kids*? Come and have a beer with us."

But Armin stayed with the children.

After a couple of hours he went home to get to bed on time.

Waltraud continued to dominate her son, bossing him in front of the few guests who went round to their house for afternoon coffee, though visitors were few, as Waltraud didn't have any close friends.

That changed when Germany's most famous witch moved in next door.

Ulla von Bernus, a self-avowed witch and satanist who published occult tracts and gave interviews to German print and broadcast media about her prowess at "casting death spells with reliability," moved into the house next door and lived there for seventeen years, between 1968 and 1985. The witch, who chose to be called by the more glamorous von Bernus rather than her real name Dannenberge, became Waltraud's best friend; soon the two were in and out of each other's house all the time.

Ulla von Bernus coated the walls of her farmhouse in thick black paint. A skull's head, out of which popped a tongue, served as a doorbell on the black-painted front door. She decorated her walls with pictures of Lucifer and erected an altar to Satan, complete with a black mirror, a dagger and candles. The farm was dubbed the "witch's house" by the locals, who still called Armin's house the "haunted house." Ulla would stand on her doorstep, with a Dunhill cigarette hanging between her deep red lips, and invite Armin and his mother into her home. She cast deep stares at them from beneath a wig of curls and waved her hands, heavy with rings, when she spoke.

Ulla preferred to be known as a "satanic priestess" rather than a witch. The divorcée held satanic masses in her black-painted room with its homemade altar. Her power, she claimed, gave her the ability to send people to their death. "I kill whenever Satan orders," she said. And according to Ulla, she nearly always succeeded. "I have a ninety percent success rate."

The satanic priestess charged between 300 and 1,000 marks to conveniently get rid of people via fatal car crashes or accidents down stairs, or so Ulla claimed. Her client base was comprised mainly of desperate women who wanted to sentence errant husbands to death. She also attracted women who wanted to kill husbands who "weren't nice to them anymore" and who were reluctant to get a divorce "for financial reasons."

Von Bernus was inundated with calls from women and men from throughout Germany who were eager to reap revenge on unfaithful spouses. She was fussy about whom she selected as a client, though. And as far as she was concerned, those she banished into eternal damnation were those who deserved it, such as sexual criminals. "I'm categorically in favor of the death penalty," she said. "I have sent twenty men to eternal damnation via a ritual distance killing," she further stated. "I bewitched them to death. And each time I made it look like an accident."

She also made use of her magical means to reunite and separate people, as well as resolve other problems, or so she claimed in her brochure. All for the appropriate fee, of course.

"My hexes and spell casting are superior to all others," von Bernus claimed. "I can help you achieve anything you want; just tell me what you need done and through my extremely powerful spell work it will be done immediately. I get the job done using my own method of black magic. Come to me with any problem and be rid of it tomorrow."

Her reputation gained strength after the three judges heading a court case suffered from heart attacks, and the prosecutor in the case was fatally injured. The accused, a child murderer, had once been a neighbor of Ulla's and rumor spread that she had used her powers to help. She made the headlines in the early 1980s when she was taken to court by a disgruntled woman who said she had paid Ulla 3,000 marks to put a death curse on her husband, who then did not die. The court ruled that Frau von Bernus was guilty of an "illusory crime exempt from punishment" and ordered her to repay the money. The court in Kassel judged that the whole business "had been objectively impossible from the start."

When not summoning people to an early grave, von Bernus spent her time at the roulette table at the casino in Bad Harzburg. Satan didn't tell her the winning numbers, though. "He has more important things to do."

Armin quickly fell under his new neighbor's spell. She told the teenager how she was in contact with extraterrestrial beings. She sparked his imagination with tales of anthropomorphic beings with cloven hooves, a barbed tail and horns. "Atlantis is going to reappear," she said. But "the world will soon disappear into chaos." She also told him her dreams. "I would like to appear on a talk show with the pope to discuss it all," she said.

As far as von Bernus was concerned, humans were animals; nature was uncaring and part of its natural process was death. She saw Satan as the dark force in nature and she wanted him to replace God. She worshipped this "dark force" and Satan's qualities. Whenever Armin popped next door for a coffee and a chat, he was instructed in the religion of a world ruled by Satan, of the flesh, the carnal, and of death.

And so he was exposed to a role model apart from his domineering mother. Armin had found a real-life witch to bring alive his beloved tale of Hansel and Gretel. His witch didn't live in a house with a gingerbread roof, or marzipan windows, but she was just as good.

Eventually, money difficulties forced Ulla to sell her house in Rotenburg to Guenther Hoepfner and move to an apartment in Bad Harzburg, south of Hanover, to spend more time playing roulette in the casino.

Even after Ulla moved away, her influence over Armin remained.

Since meeting her, his dreams had been dipped in tinges of black magic. The occult exercised its influence over his weak personality and encouraged him to pursue his dark desires. He started to act out his savage fantasies. He dismembered Barbie dolls as if they were real victims. He cooked their severed limbs on the barbecue in the garden. The dolls' smiling faces disintegrated between the metal bars; their bright, cheerful colors melted into a black charcoal mess. Legs and arms dissolved under the heat of the barbecue and dripped through to the grill pan below.

Armin created more dolls to play with after he barbecued the Barbies. He made these dolls himself, out of marzipan from his mother's supplies, and spent hours modeling them into lifelike forms. It was more fun than modeling houses, he thought. Particularly when he ripped the sweet dolls to shreds. His sexuality started to influence his games. He molded the shape of his penis in marzipan and stared at it in fascination. His artistry also included human-shaped marzipan hearts, livers and stomachs. They all tasted good to him.

Armin's culinary experiments then extended to meat.

At night he made bizarre arrangements out of pork and ketchup, trying to simulate scenes of torn flesh covered in blood. He took photos and videos of his work and carefully locked them away.

Not out of shame; he didn't think he was doing anything wrong.

He hid them out of fear of his mother's reaction.

4

Armin's Life as a Young Man

Armin's choice of career after he graduated from high school was an obvious one: he joined the military. He was eighteen years old and used to obeying orders and living a regimented lifestyle. His mother had ordered him around the house like a drill sergeant all his life—now it was someone else's turn. Eager to please and keen to obey, he easily fell into the rhythms of army life. Armin became a conscientious and committed military man who regularly turned up ten minutes early to work and volunteered for extra shifts.

Armin's obedience served him well. After joining the military as a noncommissioned officer, he moved up the ranks to become an administrative clerk, before progressing to take on the responsibilities of staff sergeant in the Supplies Division of the 52nd Armored Infantry Battalion. He worked in an office role, ordering all the supplies that his battalion needed.

During his twelve years as a noncommissioned officer in ordnance, Armin gained a reputation for being quiet, calm and having impeccable manners. His solitary ways also led him to be known as a loner and "weird." Armin didn't have any hobbies, nor did he join in playing football with the other men in the evenings. He preferred to keep his own company. He rarely spent money on trips away from the base, apart from when he was invited to go sailing with people he knew from the region. Armin was a good sailor who volunteered to do as much as he could on the boat, rushing to wash the deck and hoist the sail before the others had a chance. The first time he went sailing, he told his mother he had to go away on a military excursion. The second time he went along, he asked his mother's permission to go and rang her every second day from the boat to check in.

While Armin's mother had trained her son well for a life of discipline and receiving orders, she hadn't given him any experience at being in a position of leadership. As a sergeant, Armin had ten officers and two civil employees working under him. Yet he lacked the necessary toughness to be a superior officer and failed to assert his authority over them. Soon those lower down the chain of command were bossing him around. Armin approved every soldier's request to finish his shift early. When one of his inferior's sons got married, Armin volunteered to work as a waiter at the wedding and serve him and the other guests. He felt more comfortable in the role of servant than that of master.

In the evenings, Armin slipped back into the role of a submissive son.

His battalion was stationed in Rotenburg most of the time, so he could go home to his mother nearly every night. His mother even accompanied him on troop outings in the early 1980s. They shared a double room whenever the troops spent the night away. His army mates found it all somewhat strange. "Armin, you're such a mama's boy," Wolfgang, one of the officers, teased. "Does she make you wash behind your ears before you go to bed? Do you have to ask her permission to go to the toilet too?" "Armin, do we have to check with your mother for orders or with you?" another laughed. "Don't you think you're old enough to spend a night away from your mummy? Good God, man, you're not seven anymore."

But Armin brushed off all the mockery. He didn't care.

At the officers' Christmas party, the soldiers proudly walked into the garland-decorated hall, showing off their wives or latest girlfriends. The women had spent weeks shopping for the right outfit and had been fixing their hair and makeup all afternoon. They invested in hair spray, nail polish and shoulder pads to create their look. The single women spent the evening vying for the soldiers' attention and flirting with the best-looking and most eligible officers in the hall.

Armin invited his mother to the party and spent the evening by her side.

This was not unusual. On his rare dates with women, she chaperoned. Waltraud would sit in the backseat of the car, listening in to the girls' conversations with her son, her face frozen in a pained expression. She waited in the car for them if they went out for something to drink, ready to assert her control over her dutiful son as soon as they returned.

Armin couldn't understand why his potential girlfriends found it so odd. Why shouldn't his mother be there too? They didn't expect him to leave his mother at home alone with no one to talk to, surely? He was perplexed that girls wanted to be alone with him. After all, his mother *had* to go everywhere he went, didn't she?

Waltraud was determined to be the number one woman in Armin's life. She wasn't going to let any other female wrestle away her last male companion. She dismissed the few girls Armin brought back to the house. "She's simply not suitable," she said. "She's not good enough for you, Armin. You can't be seen with someone as common as that. Did you hear the way she talked? Her enunciation is atrocious." The next one was "too bossy." Another girl was "too plain." There was always plenty for her to find fault with in any of her son's potential girlfriends. Armin took every word to heart.

He also knew that his mother would be more than disapproving if he brought a male "friend" to the house. She simply wouldn't tolerate it, wouldn't accept that any son of hers was gay, so he kept his homosexual feelings well under wraps. He never came out or openly declared a relationship with a male partner. Indeed, most people who knew him had no idea he was gay. He wasn't even sure himself. No one had ever told him he was, and sometimes he found it difficult to trust his own opinion. "Do you think I'm a homosexual?" he once asked his neighbor Manfred, who served in the army with him.

"That's something you must know yourself, Armin," Manfred replied

Armin kept quiet. He didn't want to talk about it anymore. He knew he wanted a wife someday so he could have children, but he also knew that it was men he was sexually attracted to. It was easier for him to do without a relationship with either a man or a woman. He wasn't sure how to get close to either of the sexes. And besides he always had his mother.

While his peers took their girlfriends out at the weekends, Armin, at the age of twenty-eight, was taking his mother on dates. On Sunday afternoons, they went out in their old, yellow Mercedes and drove around the region in their Sunday best. It was the highlight of the week for both of them. Waltraud got dressed up in a traditional

Bavarian dirndl dress with a plunging neckline, put on her finest jewelry, colored her cheeks with rouge and painted her lips red. Armin, meanwhile, would wear a suit to accompany his "lady." It was an image straight out of the 1950s. Even the neighbors, who were used to Armin and his mother's strange ways, were taken by surprise. .

"Why don't you ask a girl out?" Karl-Friedrich Schnaar asked Armin when he went to buy some eggs at the Schnaar's farm next door one Sunday.

Armin just shrugged his shoulders.

In the early 1990s, Waltraud was seriously hurt in a car crash, and was no longer able to do much by herself. Armin was there for her every need, and mother and son became even more reliant on each other.

Armin's life underwent a big change when he was forced to leave the army in 1991.

He wanted to stay on and remain within the safe confines of the military, but they didn't want him. He may have been a diligent officer, but he would never make a leader or be good at commanding men. His future lay elsewhere.

Armin attended a course to be retrained as a computer technician and started looking for jobs. He was taken on as a service technician for Fiducia, a software firm in the Rhine Valley city of Karlsruhe, three hundred kilometers south of Rotenburg. He worked at one of their subsidiaries in Kassel. His main job was servicing automatic cash machines for the Raiffeisenbank chain of banks. He also overhauled their computers, printers and other office equipment. "You're hardworking, technically skilled and get the job done," Armin's boss praised him at his annual review.

Armin's days were spent driving around the region, servicing machines.

It suited him fine; machines were far easier to deal with than human beings.

Armin was reserved with his office colleagues. He attended the annual Christmas parties and standard office events but otherwise avoided his workmates. The other technicians didn't think that much of it; they were often keen to get home too, to their loving wives and children after a hard day's work. And Armin had his mother to look after. Some of his evenings *were* spent in the sauna with a colleague—but Armin was far more interested in feasting his eyes on naked male flesh than being sociable. Here he was given free range to gaze at the torsos of naked men and let his eyes linger on their biceps, glistening with sweat.

Armin enjoyed his daily work. Most of all, he loved the anonymity of computers. His job provided him with a perfect opportunity to separate himself from others. He loved the complexity of the machines, and as his computer knowledge grew, he became skilled at programming, games and surfing the Net. He began to dream of one day being self-employed. He wanted to renovate the Rotenburg farmhouse and turn it into a residential computer school, where executives could stay and attend week-long computer courses. His brother, Ingbert, who worked at IT in Frankfurt, could help him, Armin thought. His other ambition was to set up an Internet company for pharmaceuticals.

Excited by his plans, Armin started doing up the house.

He bought some bathroom tiles to try and modernize one of the old-fashioned bathrooms. When the first batch of red tiles ran out, he went and bought some more. But this time he decided he preferred black tiles. By the time he had finished, he had four different color tiles covering the walls of the bathroom. That was typical of Armin—he could never make up his mind or take things to their conclusion. So his plans remained dreams and nothing more. He lacked the courage to carry them through; he also didn't have enough money to properly renovate the house.

Armin took home about 3,000 marks per month. He bought old cars with his wages and left them parked on the lawn and in need of repair. He collected a Wartburg, an old Mercedes-Benz 108 and two Trabants—a personal carrier that emerged out of East Germany in the late 1950s. Armin always intended to fix them up but never got around to it. The cars stayed in the yard, parked next to an old parking sign marked with a large letter "P," keeping an old Ford Escort company. Armin collected other junk that now cluttered up the yard. Parts of old lawnmowers with broken engines, heaps of old tires, a cement mixer and an office chair began to pile up among the weeds.

He did invest some of his monthly wages on suits, shirts and ties—his mother had drilled into him how important appearances were, and he wanted to look smart at work. She had groomed him to become a gentleman, and his manners were impeccable. To anyone who met him, Armin appeared to be a shy, well-brought-up and harmless young man.

Of course, they couldn't see inside his head to glimpse his growing appetite for destruction.

5

The Impact
of His
Mother's
Death

Waltraud died in her bed after a long illness on September 2, 1999, at the age of seventy-seven.. Armin was thirty-seven years old. "It's terrible. Now I'm all alone in the world," he told colleagues. "I felt the moment when Mother passed away," he said. "I wasn't at home when she died, but I felt something tense up inside."

Armin's two half-brothers came back for the funeral. The eldest brother was by now a parish priest; the other worked in computers. They left again after a few days.

And suddenly Armin was on his own.

After nearly forty years of living with his mother, Armin went home to an empty house.

His pony was dead, and so was his pet Alsation. He bought an expensive Persian cat, Cleo, for company. The cat wandered around the farm and occasionally acknowledged her owner. Armin felt lonely. He turned the home he had shared with his late mother into a shrine devoted to her memory. Like Norman Bates, the motel manager in Alfred Hitchcock's thriller *Psycho,* Armin started imagining he *was* his mother, wearing her dresses and impersonating her voice. He fastidiously cleaned her room, her silverware and her hairbrushes like she always had. One day, he startled his old school friend Berthold Sieberg by opening the door wearing his mother's floral frock, makeup and wig.

"He's taken over his mother's role in the house," Berthold gossiped afterward. "I had a real shock when I went into her room," he said. "Her dressing gown was laid out neatly on the bed, beautifully pressed, as if he's expecting her back any moment. His world's frozen in the time when she was still alive. It's spooky. Armin has become his mother."

Apart from his mother's room, Armin didn't bother cleaning the house.

It was too big and no one was there to appreciate his efforts.

Instead he began living mainly on the ground floor, where the walls were covered with swords and shields, which his mother had used as decoration. There was a lounge, a dining room with a large table, and a kitchen. Nearly every other room, apart from those three on the ground floor, was furnished with a bed and a television set. Armin still dreamt of renovating the house and turning it into a residential computer center or hotel—which he now planned to sell for one million marks. But the farmhouse remained badly in need of loving care. Layers of dust and cobwebs gathered in the corners of the abandoned rooms. The cellar swam under water and became a breeding ground for rats.

Armin occasionally asked his neighbors over for coffee or for dinner. There was Guenther Hoepfner, who lived thirty meters away in Ulla's old house; Friedrich and Gertrude Baunack, whose house was about one hundred meters away; as well as Joerg and Ella Paulussen, who lived about two hundred meters away. Manfred Stück's house and Karl-Friedrich Schnaar's farm lay one hundred meters behind Armin's estate.

To the village residents, Meiwes seemed like a good neighbor. It annoyed them that his house was a mess, but their attitude was *Well, what can you do about it?* Besides, he was always ready to help out. He mowed their lawns, fixed their computers and helped them chop wood. At Christmas he even played Santa Claus for their children. The locals saw him as an awkward, peculiar man who was nevertheless extremely polite, well-presented and clean-shaven, who always smiled a broad grin at them from under dark, blond hair. It was difficult for them to know *what* to talk to him about, but they readily offered their help after his mother died. "Armin, if you're ever in bad way now that your mother has passed on, then come over and talk to us about it," his neighbor Karl-Friedrich said. "We're there for you if you need us." But Armin never took up his offer, or those from other neighbors. They found it strange; how could Armin expect to heal his wounds if he didn't talk to anyone about his problems or feelings? Armin did get help from one neighbor: he didn't realize he had to insure his car until this neighbor pointed it out.

Armin still attended the regular village barbecues and summer parties, and occasionally took part in the villagers' political debates. But he wasn't a good sparring partner. He switched opinions depending on whom he was speaking to. Other debaters found him weak, instable and easy to manipulate. When it came to men's talk about women and sex, he was simply awkward. "Yes of course, I've tried it all often enough," he said to Karl-Friedrich on one such occasion, and then lit up a cigarette and fell silent.

Armin found it easier to talk to the children than their

parents. Sometimes his neighbors' sons came round to play. Armin would light a fire in the hearth in the evenings, and barbecue the meat that the boys brought with them. Often they watched TV together. But the children weren't allowed to watch "anything violent." The parents in this very rural, trusting community trusted Armin with their children. They considered him a bit strange but ultimately harmless. They had no idea of his darker side; he never let them see it.

Armin increasingly longed to have his own family, to fill up his house with the laughter and chaos of lots of children. He wanted to recreate the type of childhood and home life he felt he had missed out on. When an acquaintance in Wüstefeld moved away, she gave him her pink-and-lilac-colored swing set, and he erected it in the farmhouse garden. His kids could play on it one day, he figured, and smiled to himself. The swing slowly rusted away, unused.

In 1996, Nicole Svetek moved into the Schnaars' farmhouse extension. She lived there with her three children and her boyfriend until 2001. Armin enjoyed spending evenings with the family. "I can see you feel at home here with us and the children," Nicole said to him. "You're like a big kid yourself, Armin! The way you play with the kids."

Armin grew particularly close to Nicole's two sons. He helped Elia, the eldest son, learn how to drive, and played with Jakob, the younger son, on his model railway set, the one his mother set up in the attic. Elia often went round to Armin's house; he and Armin would sit in front of Armin's computer and play games, shooting moorhens dead.

Armin urged the Sveteks to move into his house so he could surround himself with a ready-made family. His new family would include the boyfriend if need be, he conceded. They didn't take him up on his offer. After five years, they moved out of Rotenburg, and Armin's life.

Armin had joined a marriage institute in late 1999 to find a wife to settle down with. But, not surprisingly, he didn't have any luck. He came across as a quiet, unassuming computer nerd; his contact with women was eventually reduced to evenings spent in the Blue Moon brothel in Kassel. There he ate, drank and fell asleep on the bar but never picked up any of the prostitutes.

And then one evening later that year things took a turn for the better.

Armin's reserved and polite ways won over a woman named Karin. She found this quiet man who was tall and slim with an athletic build to be quite good-looking. At last, Armin thought, *someone he could maybe share his life with*! His thoughts raced ahead of themselves. He decided he'd take her back home and show her where they could one day build their family.

"I'm not going to move in there," she told him as soon as she saw his ramshackle, musty home. There was no way she could be persuaded otherwise, she told him. Absolutely none. But there was equally no way Armin would move out of his mother's manor house. The romance ended as quickly as it had started.

Marion Reich, an acquaintance from Rotenburg who he used to walk his dog with, decided to take matters into her own hands. "Armin, you need a girlfriend," she declared. Marion paired Armin off with a young woman called Martina on New Year's Eve 1999. Martina was thirty-six, pleasant, and what's more, she had three children. She was won over by Armin's manners, and the way he had with her kids. She was delighted that he spent hours joining them in the secret world of make-believe. They began to date. They went to the disco together; they held hands when they went for walks.

"You and the children are the dearest people to me," Armin wrote in a love letter to Martina, in January 2000.

"A mother that thinks of her children first is the best and most beautiful woman in the world." Martina bought Armin a magician doll as a present and enclosed a letter: "You enchant me," it read.

Armin now had something to boast about to his colleagues. He placed a photo of a smiling Martina on his desk and bragged that he was engaged. In reality, he had only given her a ring as a present. He also boasted that he had slept with Martina, but this too was untrue. Martina kept thick tights on in bed, literally, as she didn't want to fall pregnant again. When Martina told Armin that she was going to be sterilized, that she didn't want to have any more children, he was disillusioned. "If I get married, I want a fully functioning, fertile woman who can bear me children," he told her. She broke off contact when he confessed his homosexual leanings. Their friendship, the closest thing to a proper relationship Armin had ever experienced, had lasted just three weeks.

Even during his romantic adventures, Armin never broke away from his first true love—his mother. Nor did his mother's almighty dominance entirely pass away with her. Armin assumed some of her authoritarian characteristics after she died, and he often surprised people with a new, despotic side to his personality, and an overbearing air whenever things didn't go his way.

Always a conscientious employee, Armin still turned up for work on time every day wearing an ironed shirt and a dutiful expression. As soon as the working day was over, though, he retreated into a dreamworld filled with fantasies and images that nourished his cannibalistic appetites. His desire to kill someone grew stronger after his mother's death, and his cannibalistic fantasies became more concrete and more brutal.

He started to research the world of cannibalism and its long-standing roots in human behavior. He was delighted to discover that ancient humans regularly devoured the flesh of other people—so he wasn't the only one with the urge to consume a fellow human being! He learned that the term "cannibalism" derived from the name of the West Indian Carib tribe, first documented by the explorer Christopher Columbus. The Carib tribe was alleged to supplement their fruit and fish diet with human flesh. He read how the Fore, an isolated tribe of people in Papua New Guinea, engaged in ritualistic funeral feasts from the late nineteenth century until cannibalism was banned in the 1950s. And about the Aztecs, who practiced cannibalism on a large scale as part of the ritual religious sacrifice of war captives and other victims in a practice known as "exocannibalism"—the eating of strangers or enemies.

He learned that other primitive people ate their enemies for their qualities as much as nutrition. They believed they could incorporate the person they had eaten and take on their characteristics. Aboriginal Australians indulged in a more "benevolent" form of cannibalism—endocannibalism—the consumption of friends and relatives who were usually already dead.

Armin devoured the book *Alive*—the tale of a Uruguayan rugby team that resorted to "survival cannibalism" after their plane crashed on the Argentinian side of the Chilean border. He also read that cannibalism was frequently used as a means to demonize others: medieval Christian culture depicted the Jew who had a taste for the blood of Christian babies.

In Armin's view, cannibalism had a quasi-religious component.

Weren't some cannibals simply recycling the bodies of dead friends and relatives into the living? Christians celebrated a metaphorical consumption of the Savior's body and blood, he thought.

Ingestion was also a symbol for sex as well as sacrament, Armin discovered.

Lovers bite each other, he reasoned. In Armin's mind, sexual cannibalism was the highest form of intimate behavior. He thought he could find in cannibalism the kind of intimacy that he had yet to find with another human.

Armin also read books about particular cannibals. He learned about Jeffrey Dahmer, the legendary serial murderer and cannibal who admitted at his trial in July 1992 to killing and eating seventeen people in the United States. Police raiding Dahmer's apartment found severed heads in the fridge, skulls in the filing cabinet and body parts in a kettle. When they discovered a human heart in the deep freeze, Dahmer explained, "I was saving it for later."

He began to tape television programs about the Vietnam War and its victims, and about Fritz Haarmann, nicknamed the "Monster of Hanover," who murdered at least twenty-four boys between 1918 and 1924. Haarmann, a butcher by trade, then sold their flesh to customers seeking cheap meat.

He read about the last alleged case of cannibalism in Germany, when a thirty-three-year-old man claimed at his robbery and murder trial in 1995 that he had eaten the innards of his victim.

He researched the life of Albert Fish, called "America's Bogeyman," who raped, murdered and ate at least fifteen children during the 1920s. Armin was interested to learn that Fish claimed to have experienced immense sexual pleasure as a result. Fish wrote to the mother of his final victim, a ten-year old girl, six years after she had vanished: "Grace sat on my lap and kissed me. I made up my mind to eat her."

He reread the tale of the German Adolph Luetgert, one

of Chicago's master butchers of the 1870s, whose driving ambition was to make his sausages famous all over America. Luetgert's dream came true. He was arrested and tried for the murder of his wife Louisa after disposing of her corpse by melting it down in one of his giant vats and incorporating her into his sausage line. For two years after Luetgert's conviction, sausage sales in Illinois and neighboring Michigan hit an all-time low.

Armin especially loved the story of the Donner party. In the winter of 1846–7, a group of American frontier settlers survived being trapped in Sierra Nevada snows by eating their dead. Two-thirds of the men died. Single adult men died first. The children died second. Male children more than female. The women died last and fewest. The story reinforced Armin's view of the necessity of women. He would never eat a woman, he decided. "Women are too important for the survival of mankind," he later said. "Sperm from a man can be frozen and used to give birth to children after his death. But women are irreplaceable for the continuity of mankind." But Armin was less judgmental about the killing of men: "To me, there's no big difference if a pig or a human being is slaughtered," he declared.

The more Armin read, the more he justified his cannibalistic urges to himself; he had finally found some new idols to replace his mother.

His research encouraged him to explore his lust for human meat. He cut out pictures of arms, legs and torsos from catalogues and glued them to a drawing of a barbecue. He took photos of his own body parts and imagined them served as choice chops or cutlets. He bought a video camera and started filming himself at home. He held a knife to his throat and smeared his body in tomato ketchup seasoned with paprika to make it look thicker, like "real blood." He took photos of his penis sandwiched between two slices of bread, with ketchup serving as blood. He garnished the dish with parsley.

Armin made a penis out of pork and placed his own member next to it on a breadboard. He continued to act out injuries and abuse on puppets and dolls made of marzipan. He also modeled life-size genitalia out of marzipan, before building an entire body out of marzipan, sprinkled with cocoa powder. Armin liked the chocolate taste.

Slaughter scenes from pornographic videos and photos collected from hard-core magazines aroused him. He started masturbating to the images. But instead of assuaging his urges, it made him want more.

6

Looking for
a Well-Built
Man
for Slaughter

It was 3.30 A.M. and Armin was still online, absorbed in the images flashing across his computer screen. He was scrolling through sadomasochism pages on the Internet. He wanted to search for more violent scenes before going to bed. It was hard to break away. The pull of the pornographic images was powerful.

The neighbors noticed that the light in his study burned late into the night. They presumed that he had difficulty sleeping. Armin knew he shouldn't tell his neighbors or anyone else how captivated he was by his online bedtime reading.

Armin saved photos and filed them away neatly during the evenings. In a folder marked "*Grausam*" (Terror), he collected photos of accident scenes and the severed body parts of their victims. In a file labeled "*Fleisch*" (Meat), he gathered pictures of raw meat. He saved images of bestiality and torture. He always kept a videocassette in the video player in case there was a bloody accident on the news, so he could record images of dead bodies. He also recorded TV footage of autopsies and developed contacts in the world of snuff videos, in which people were killed in front of live cameras. Soon he had over fifty violent videos in his collection.

But Armin's life had truly took on new purpose after he set up home Internet access.

Anonymous and accessible and only about twenty-five dollars a month, it offered an alluring arena for his compulsive sexual urges and gave him the perfect opportunity to engage in his preferred fantasies without the distraction of reality. Now he could find *hundreds* of photographs, stories and chat channels twenty-four hours a day, every day of the year.

At last, Armin had found a hobby.

Over the next five years after his mother's death, using two computers in his study, Armin saved thousands of pornographic images depicting acts of violence, torture and cannibalism. He accumulated more than fifty slaughter stories and documents on the computers' hard drives. These included essays promoting cannibalism as a way of lessening overpopulation in the Third World, and tips on the best slaughter methods for both humans and animals. His personal recipe collection now included adventurous dishes, which had been pulled off cannibal sites, such as "Panierte Jungenleber" (Boy's Liver in Breadcrumbs), and "Penis mit Rotwein" (Penis in Red Wine).

Armin's exploration of the shadowy side of the Internet proved to him there was nothing in the world that couldn't be part of sexual arousal. Necrophiliacs, sadists and masochists were all out there. Armin also realized that he could now be in contact with the whole world, anonymously.

His weakness, though, remained human flesh.

There were as many as 800,000 Web sites devoted to cannibalism for him to look at. Each one helped alleviate his feelings of loneliness and alienation. The more he read about cannibalism, the more he integrated it into his personal fantasies. He adopted the name of his imaginary friend, Franky, as his online pseudonym, and "Franky" soon became an active member of the Internet scene. He even wrote a short story entitled "*Der Strichjunge*," or "The Rent Boy," and published it online. The story was a detailed description of the killing of a prostitute, and was a progression from the violent fairy stories Armin had created as a child.

"I only have you and I only want you," said the prostitute in the story. "Let me become a part of you."

"Well that isn't right," the protagonist replied. "I'll eat you up then."

"Then slaughter me," the prostitute said. "Apart from you, nobody else is interested in me anyhow."

"But I love you!" the protagonist replied.

"And that's precisely why you have to do it or otherwise I'll kill myself," the rent boy said. "I can feel an incredible feeling inside of me, it's as if our souls are connected."

The rent boy had a "handsome male chest" and "delicious, firm, and juicy" flesh, Armin wrote. He detailed the "big, hot jets of blood" that pulsated out of the prostitute's chest when he was stabbed to death.

Armin felt proud to see his story published. He was becoming bolder as his appetite for cannibalism grew. He decided to log on to online cannibal newsgroups in search of someone to eat. He also started to engage in sexual conversation with cannibals online. After work, he hung out in

chat rooms such as the Cannibal Cafe, Gourmet, Guy
Canni-bals, Torturenet and DolcettGirls. Here humans
were described as long pigs and as cows, and preferences
for slaughter were discussed. People also swapped helpful
tips, such as "How to Practice Safe Cannibalism."

Armin learned from the chat rooms that there were
many others in the world who said they wanted to consume
and be consumed. There were several hundred people with
cannibalistic tendencies in Germany alone, and many
thousands more around the world. Armin participated in
about 430 cannibal Web sites and chat rooms, mainly with
people from Western Europe and America. He chatted with
those who wanted to slaughter, those who wanted to be
killed, potential assistants to a slaughter and those who
hadn't quite made up their minds which role they wanted
to play. And in the manner of the Internet, they conversed
freely, enjoying the frisson of talking about things that
were very, very naughty.

This was "Lonely Hearts" with a gruesome twist.

For the first time in his life, Armin met others who
seemed just like him. He found a place where he wasn't
alone, and conversed with all types of cannibal wannabes—
dentists, teachers, cooks, handymen, as well as government officials. The flourishing online cannibal scene involved middle-class professionals as well as manual
laborers. These were suburban cannibals who had opened
up their flesh-eating desires using the Internet as the key,
people from the middle reaches of society that were thirsty
for human blood. Armin often smiled to himself as he
walked down the street during his lunch break. The unassuming bank-clerk who just walked by might be the man
who'd told him of his yearnings for male flesh during a
chat exchange last night!

It was just a game for many of the chat-room participants.

Armin, however, took it all very seriously. He even set up his own cannibal chat room on Yahoo. He became Webmaster of the Internet platform where he could publish his stories and views. The online exchanges flowed as he and his bloodthirsty pen pals disclosed their innermost urges. One man told Armin during a chat exchange that he liked to go to slaughterhouses and imagine that it was humans who were being killed. Another correspondent admitted that his fantasy was to be killed and eaten by a woman; to satisfy him, Armin set up a new e-mail account and pretended to be a woman.

"I am a tall, stocky long pig looking for a big-bodied male chef, who would like to have a feast of me," said one would-be victim, using his Hotmail address.

"Helleater," meanwhile, told others that he dreamt of "being BBQed on a large grill (till it's so hot for me)."

Lisa, who nicknamed herself "Snuffy," announced she was "looking for a real sadist and cannibal, who will torture me over a long period, things like cutting off my toes and fingers . . . remove my teeth, that I can't bite you . . . And much, much more . . ." The twenty-two-year old told her readers that she could "travel everywhere" to have her desires met.

"Stevo" sent a post entitled, "my meat is urs to eat." "This message is to anyone out there, male or female, who wishes to have me as their dream meal. I am 18 years old and have tender, delicious flesh that is begging to be devoured. If you think you would like me in your belly then send me a message and I will answer all of those who explain how they will eat me."

Franky promptly replied to the post in his imperfect English. "Hi Stevo, I am Franky from Germany. I am very interested in you, tell me more about you, high, wight . . . I will butchering and eating you delicious flesh."

"Tufke" from Den Haag sent an e-mail from his Hotmail address. "If anyone wants to eat an 18 yr old gorgeous male by any means you wish, then just tell me how you would feel whilst devouring my horny flesh into ur belly and i will reply to you so we can discuss real arrangements, please eat me!"

Tufke's post attracted Armin's interest. "Hi, I am Franky from Germany. I will eat you. Please tell me your high and wight, also send me a Pic from you. Where are you from? I hope you can come quick to me, I am a hungry Cannibal. Your butcher, Franky."

Encouraged by what he was reading, Armin decided it was time for a bit of self-publicity. He wrote sixty advertisements in the personal columns of the cannibal forums using his pseudonym Franky and his e-mail address, *antrophagus@hotmail.com*. *Antrophagus* meant "cannibal" and was taken from the Greek, *anthropophagos*. The ads were entitled "Search for a young boy" or "Search boys for butchering."

"Hi, ich bin Franky aus Deutschland, ich suche nach jungen Maennern zwischen 18 und 30 Jahren, zum schlachten," ran one of Armin's ads. *"Hast du eine normal gebauten Koerper, dann komme zu mir, ich schlachte dich und esse dein koestliches Fleisch."*

Armin then attempted to translate his ad into English:

I am Franky from Germany and i search for a young
Boy, between 18 and 30 y/o. Have you a normal build
body and will you di, than come to me, i butchering
you and eat your horny flesh.

His other ads contained a similar message: "Looking for a young, well-built man, who wants to be eaten by me. Detailed photos desired." Or: "Looking for a well-built man, 18–30 years old, for slaughter." Other ads followed: "Gay male seeks hunks 18–30 for slaughter."

Armin got his first reply. A "Matteo" said that he wanted to be tortured, killed and eaten by Franky. A woman contacted him asking to be slaughtered but he turned her down; he wanted to eat a man not a woman. He was looking for a man over eighteen who would be killed willingly. Replies from others followed. They called themselves "*Schlachtjunge,*" or "Butcherboy"; "*Maedchenfleisch,*" or "Girls' flesh", or simply, "Meat4food." Respondents including "Hannibal Lektor," "bbq-meat," "scalloped2," or the aptly christened "eatmefordinner" also responded to Armin's post. They were all young men who were aroused by the thought of human flesh and who wanted to arrange to have themselves slaughtered like animals for a turn-on.

Armin's nights became busy as he answered e-mail correspondence from the people who wrote to volunteer to be his meal. In the end, *204* offered themselves up for his consumption. In addition, thirty were ready to do the slaughtering, and a further fifteen merely wanted to watch.

Armin calmly set about interviewing the applicants.

He arranged approximately thirty meetings to get to know his possible victims. He drove to the German cities of Dresden and Hamburg, and as far as the Netherlands, in his quest. He also asked his new friends to travel and see him. But all of the meetings fell through. Only a tiny portion of those entering cannibal chat rooms were willing to follow through and meet in real life.

In July 2000, Armin got to know "Jörg" from Villingen Schwenningen. The thirty-one year old hotel cook offered up his colleagues as potential meals. He and Armin exchanged e-mails discussing how they could stun the young men with a hammer and then chop up their bodies.

"Boys' stomachs, stuffed with mincemeat, is a good dish," said Jörg.

"I can hardly wait until I can taste the tender flesh on my tongue," Franky replied.

Armin hoped that Jörg would offer himself up for slaughter, as he sounded like an ideal slaughter boy. He was also worried that Jörg's colleagues wouldn't want to end up as meals.

"Did you kill any young men over the holidays?" Jörg asked.

"It was the only thing I didn't do over the holidays," replied Franky. "Do you think that I have slipped out, that I want to kill a young man and eat him?" continued Franky in his poor English, teasing that he might have jeopardized their plans by letting them slip to an outsider.

An increasingly excited Armin persuaded Jörg to come and see him. The two met at a motel, then at a Kassel hotel and finally at the farmhouse. Armin tied up Jörg, described to him which pieces of flesh lay under his skin and marked the sections with a colored pen on Jörg's naked body. He tried time and again to convince Jörg to let him slaughter him. But all of his efforts were in vain—Jörg complained that his ankles hurt, and said no. He only wanted to act out the slaughter fantasies because it turned him on, he told Armin. He didn't want to carry them out in reality.

Armin untied Jörg and let him go.

He only wanted to kill a man who willingly gave himself up for the slaughter.

Then on February 5, 2001, Armin saw a posting unlike any other. "CATOR99" declared, "I offer myself up and will let you dine from my live body. Not butchery, dining!" Cator's note was explicit and challenging. Armin wrote back immediately to express his interest and ask for Cator's specifics. In the real world, CATOR99 was Bernd Juergen Brandes.

"I am 36 years old, 175 cm and weigh 72 kg. I hope you

are really serious about it because I really want it," Cator replied.

Armin reread the last phrase, "because I really want it." Unlike his former correspondents, Cator didn't seem to be merely playing with the sexual allure of being eaten; he seemed earnest.

"There are a lot of people out there who are interested, but only a few who really mean it," Franky wrote to Cator. "Whoever REALLY wants to do it, needs a REAL VICTIM!" Cator answered.

Armin sent Bernd torture fantasies. The two exchanged photos of each other naked. Armin also sent Bernd pictures of his teeth. "I will sink them into your body and bite off your tongue," he wrote in an e-mail.

"That won't be Hell but Heaven on earth," Bernd wrote back.

"This will be the biggest kick for me," Armin said. "I get a kick out of the idea of having another person inside me."

"Great," said Bernd.

"Terrific," replied Armin.

It all seemed so simple. Bernd wanted to be castrated and eaten; Armin wanted to eat a young man. They made an online pact to fulfill both their wishes, and arranged to meet. Bernd would come to Rotenburg on Friday, March 9, 2001. Armin could hardly wait. "This is what I was born to do," Franky said. "I will reach my life's goal at last."

"I'm your meat," Cator replied.

There was little more that needed to be said to cement the relationship. Barely one month after meeting each other over the Internet, they were to see each other in the flesh.

7

The Slaughter Room

Armin decided he needed to build a slaughter room. He was moving closer to his dream of butchering a young male for food, and he wanted to make sure he had the right instruments and surroundings to accomplish his goal.

The human being he was anticipating (referred to throughout cannibal culinary history as "long pig" and "hairless goat" in the case of younger specimens) weighed between 100 and 200 pounds. Armin read on cannibal Web sites that a "long pig" of this weight could easily be manipulated by one person. His online research also told him that the rendering of a human carcass required a fairly large amount of time, effort and space.

Armin searched his mother's house for the most suitable space to create his human abattoir. It would be on the second floor, in the farmhouse's former smokehouse, he finally decided. Armin rarely went upstairs to the second floor, nor did any of his few visitors. Locating the slaughter room on the second floor would insure that it (and the secret of its human butchery) would remain hidden from the curious eyes of any of the neighbors or colleagues who infrequently came around to the house for coffee and cake. They had no reason to go upstairs.

The abandoned smokehouse on the second floor—a common location for such a room in a large, old house like Armin's—smelled dank. Paint and plaster had peeled off the walls, revealing patches of damp. The concrete floor was cold and uninviting. The room was perfect for Armin's needs. At last motivated to carry out some renovations, he set out to create his ideal room.

His concept of decor and interior design, however, would be appreciated by few.

He adorned the killing room with meat hooks where he could hang a carcass or hunks of flesh. He then constructed a meat trough to drain the river of human blood that would flow from his victim. He dragged a rusty iron bed to the center of the room; a blue floral mattress and a quilt rested on top of the coiled metal springs. This would be the altar where Bernd would be sacrificed. Armin laid ropes and a belt on the bed so that he could tie Bernd down and restrain him, if necessary.

He arranged two bedside cabinets on either side of the mattress. In one cabinet, he kept a *Fix-und-Foxi* comic book, which narrated the mischievous adventures of two cartoon mice, loved by German children and Armin alike. In the other, he placed a lemon-scented room air freshener. He didn't want the room to smell stale. He placed two electric heaters by the bed. Armin was still corresponding with Matteo, who relayed fantasies of how he wanted to be barbecued alive. Armin wanted to make sure he could carry out Matteo's fantasy, if given the chance.

He nailed two blocks of wood on the wall to form the shape of cross. He draped life-size mannequins (bought

over the Internet) over the nails. As he carried out his renovations, Armin imagined Bernd hanging there, as naked
and vulnerable as the lifeless mannequins. He attached a
pulley to the ceiling so that he could haul Bernd up by his
feet.

An old metal patio table served as a butcher's bench.
The holes in the table would allow blood to drain through
to the concrete floor. Most of his work, Armin reasoned,
could be performed with a few simple tools such as sharp,
clean-bladed knives and his grandmother's axe, which he
fetched out of the kitchen. He arranged his slaughter instruments neatly on the table.

Armin created a whip out of parts of an old umbrella
and a TV cable. He bought a whip with nine tails from the
Beatse Uhse sex shop to ensure he could inflict sufficient
punishment on those victims that wanted it. He was particularly proud of a wooden cage that he built and placed in
the corner of the room. He thought that a sense of confinement might appeal to a potential victim. He used additional
mattresses to soundproof the room and smother any
screams of pain that might come from Bernd's lips. He
turned up the radio loud as a test and left the room. It
worked well. You couldn't hear a sound.

Armin was pleased with his renovations. He took photos of the human torture chamber, with its heaters that
could barbecue human flesh, and sent them to Matteo, hoping to entice him to visit.

Matteo didn't write back. Indeed he never replied again.

Armin e-mailed photos of the slaughter room elsewhere, and posted photos of it on the Internet. He started to
attract attention. Some would-be victims wanted to see the
room; Armin told them he would draw lines on their bodies, and mark where he could make his cuts. He continued
to scroll through cannibal chat-room postings to whet his
appetite for his meal to come. He chatted with Balu, who

urged chat-room co-habitants to "email me as I've got good slaughter flesh."

He also corresponded with "bbq-meat," who was searching for a human butcher whom he wanted to "split, cut and eat me alive." A "Gangre" told Armin and others looking at his post that he was looking "for a real chef willing to roast a male long pig alive" and asked if there was "anyone out there?" One person who responded to Armin's Internet posting pleaded with Armin to kill him. He was rejected because Armin said he was "too fatty" after seeing a photo.

Armin could choose to be fussy in his eating habits; the human race was a large herd to pick from, and he knew whom he wanted to consume. Since Bernd had confirmed his interest, Armin was confident he had his victim. Soon he would have a replacement inside him for the brother who had left home all those years ago. He would also fill the void from his mother's death. He wouldn't be alone anymore when he had eaten Bernd. What's more, he thought, he could take on Bernd's spirit and his qualities.

Armin had read that animals raised for slaughter were kept in tightly controlled environments, with their health and diet carefully maintained. Humans, of course, were not kept under such conditions. This meant that people were subject to an enormous range of diseases, infections, chemical imbalances and poisonous bad habits, including cigarettes and alcohol. Armin concluded that to get the best results from Bernd, freshness was imperative. He would have to make sure that Bernd ate no food for forty-eight hours, but drank plenty of water before coming to see him. The fasting would help flush his system, purging stored toxins and bodily wastes, and would make the job of bleeding him and cleaning him easier.

One nagging concern was Bernd's age. Bernd had told Armin he was thirty-six—past Armin's ideal "sell-by date" as far as fresh human produce was concerned. No farm animal was ever allowed to age for thirty years or more. Six to thirteen months old was a more common slaughtering point. Meat lost its tenderness as an animal aged, becoming tough and stringy. But Bernd looked physically fit and was in apparently good health. He said he worked out at the gym and his photo showed off a body that was well toned with defined muscles. Bernd also wasn't too skinny. Armin wanted his victim to have a certain amount of fat to add a juicy, flavorful quality to the meat.

At this point, Armin wasn't sure how much meat he would get from the body. He knew that a human was neither built nor bred for its meat, and so would not provide nearly as much flesh as, say, a pig or cow. An average 1,000-pound steer broke down to provide 432 pounds of saleable beef, he had read. Humans also differed from animals in the sense that their large pelvis and broad shoulder blades could interfere with achieving perfect cuts.

Armin took lessons from local animal slaughterhouses to determine the best method of slaughter. He watched (without permission) how animals at slaughterhouses were shackled together, being prodded, kicked and sworn at as they were herded down the ramps to their death. Some animals were decapitated, some were burned to death, while others were suffocated to death by having their heads buried in the ground. Armin rejected all these methods as unsuitable. He wanted Bernd to have a nice death. He wanted to release Bernd from his earthly chains and help him leave the world in the least painful way possible. He didn't want him to suffer any more than was necessary. Another slaughter method was the Halal way; their throats were slit, and they were left to bleed to death. The bleeding method was intended to cause the least possible damage to the carcass. Armin reasoned that if Bernd lost consciousness and *then* bled to death, he would feel no pain. He could kill Bernd with a stab to the throat for as humane a killing as possible.

Once his victim was dead, he would be ready to be hoisted. He would have to raise the feet up first, then the hands, with the head down—this, he'd learned, was called the "Gein Configuration." Armin would then tie simple loops of rope around the hands and feet. Bernd's legs would need to be spread, so that the feet were outside the shoulders, with the arms roughly parallel to the legs. This would provide access to the pelvis and keep the arms out of the way.

Armin now felt ready. His human abattoir was complete, and the scene was set. Most wonderfully, the date his willing accomplice would arrive was soon approaching.

8

Bernd,
the Meal

Bernd Juergen Brandes was blessed with a good start in life. He was born into a middle-class household in the lively German metropolis of Berlin, and was the son of two respected members of the medical profession. His parents wanted to give their son a good upbringing and they had the money to do so. Bernd's father was a general practitioner in the Berlin district of Zehlendorf. His mother was a practicing anaesthetist in a local hospital.

But the boy's secure, happy childhood was shattered in 1963, when he was five years old. His mother was having problems at work; one of her patients died because of a mistake she had made. She couldn't forgive herself for her professional error, so the family decided to escape on a short break to Sylt, the largest of the North Frisian Islands in the North Sea. Young Bernd loved the seaside and laughed as he built sandcastles on the beach and splashed in the waves, enjoying the sun and the fresh air. It was exciting to be away from home, and to have time to play with his parents. His mother wasn't able to enjoy herself, however. Even the idyllic location couldn't divert her mind away from her problems.

She drove into a tree during the holiday, and died.

Bernd's father never believed that the car crash was an accident. His wife had taken her own life, he often said. She couldn't cope anymore with the feelings of guilt that plagued her after her patient's death.

Bernd's world changed overnight. No longer was he protected by invincible parents: Where was his Mummy? Why wasn't she around to cuddle him and play tickling games like she used to? Where was she at night to tuck him up in bed and read him a bedtime story? Like many young children, Bernd blamed himself for his mother's disappearance. It was his fault, he decided, that his Mummy had gone away. He was responsible for her death. His father never contradicted this childish belief; in fact, he never spoke to his son about his mother's death. The child was too young to understand, he rationalized, and he didn't want to further traumatize the boy at such a tender age. So Bernd learned not to discuss his inner turmoil, or his deeper emotions, with his father; he also learned to conceal any negative emotions.

It was a lesson he never forgot.

Bernd's assumption of guilt for his mother's death left an indelible footprint on his psychological development and firmly embedded the embryo of a severe psychiatric disorder. As a young boy, he started to connect his sexuality and his genitalia with the death of his mother. The only way he could see of atoning for her fatal accident was through his own annihilation and endless suffering. Bernd started to dream of being slaughtered and eaten. This childhood preoccupation would develop into an overwhelming desire for self-destruction.

After the loss of his mother, Bernd's care and upbringing was placed in the hands of various au pair girls. Then three years after his first wife died, Bernd's father remarried. Bernd got on well with his new stepmother, as he did with most people he met. He was an amiable and easygoing boy who seemed to be free of behavioral problems. His father didn't realize that, deep down, his son was extremely troubled; he didn't catch glimpses of depression or of suicidal tendencies. Indeed, most people who knew Bernd saw him as a cheerful character, someone who loved life.

Bernd's school years progressed smoothly. The conscientious student passed his *Abitur,* or school-leaving exam, with a high grade. The next stop in his education was Berlin's technical university. His chosen subject was electrical engineering. He qualified as an engineer in 1986 with a good degree. All signs pointed toward a successful future.

Bernd had already secured a work placement at Siemens AG, Germany's largest engineering company, during his studies. He enjoyed working on computer software during his placement at the firm, and immediately applied for a job there after university. The graduate quickly won a full-time contract at the company's Berlin base. It was the start of a fifteen-year career at the engineering giant, where Bernd would test software for telephone systems and become a world specialist in his work on telecommunications.

The young graduate soon impressed his superiors. After just four years, Bernd was promoted to head of department. The eight employees who worked for him valued their boss and considered him a friendly and judicious manager. The rest of his colleagues also liked and respected the sociable, organized software developer. Bernd became known for telling jokes and having fun at the office. What's more, he really loved his subject, regularly raving about the systems he had developed.

Bernd never revealed to his fellow workers his inner distress or his wish for self-annihilation. As far as his colleagues were concerned, he was a normal employee who earned a good salary, enjoyed a bourgeois lifestyle and had a healthy social life. Bernd often chatted with his colleagues about his long-term girlfriend, Ariane. Bernd and Ariane got to know each other in 1987 via a personal ad in *TIP*, a Berlin city magazine.

It wasn't love at first sight, but the couple got on well. Ariane, who was three years younger than Bernd, told him she liked the fact that he was "a thinker, a good listener and an easygoing, domestic type." She told her friends, "He's so stable and secure."

The attraction was mutual.

"I want you to move in with me," Bernd told Ariane after a year of dating. The couple's relationship grew closer as they continued to get on well, even in the bedroom. The only thing that Ariane found strange was Bernd's relationship with his father. Father and son were cool and distant with each other. Even as an adult, Bernd never dared tell his father that he smoked. His father was vehemently anti-smoking. Bernd, meanwhile, often went through a pack of cigarettes during evenings spent in front of his computer. Bernd loved working on his PC. He even set up a computer club, known as "The Best in Town" and some 120 Berlin residents joined and got to know one another.

After a few years together, however, Bernd and Ariane started to drift apart. Somehow they didn't seem to have anything to say to each other anymore. The couple tried counseling, but it failed to resolve their problems. Bernd didn't want to discuss his feelings with the counselor. His almost seven-year relationship with Ariane, who was by now suffering from multiple sclerosis, ended in 1994. Bernd waited just three months before he started looking around for someone else.

"I just can't be on my own," he confided in Angela Hobeck, a colleague. "I'm going to start looking for a new mate."

Bernd pored over the lonely hearts ads in search of a replacement for Ariane. He started organizing dinner dates in the hope of finding a new partner. Then in October 1996, he met Petra. She was twelve years younger than Bernd, and full of fun. Bernd was always affectionate with Petra and showed her lots of attention. But their relationship couldn't survive Bernd's shocking revelation in 1998. "I have feelings for men," Bernd told his girlfriend.

Bernd's confession destroyed his romance with Petra. His romantic interests switched, instead, to Daniela. Bernd boasted to his colleagues that he tried "outrageous moves" in the bedroom with her—what he didn't admit was that they failed to satisfy his bisexual tendencies.

Bernd's love life was deteriorating. He was getting older and still hadn't found the right partner. He turned to the Internet and the online dating scene in the hope of finding someone. If necessary, Bernd thought, he would pay for the right person. After all, he earned a good wage and had money to spare. He started dating a girl over the Internet and gambled 6,000 marks to bring her over from Nigeria. But when he turned up at the airport to meet her, she wasn't there. Instead, he met another man who had fallen for the same trick.

Bernd was furious. His colleagues, meanwhile, found it difficult not to laugh.

"I'm going to fly over there and find out where my money has gone," Bernd angrily told one of his colleagues, Stefan Pommerening.

Bernd placed more personal ads. His efforts paid off

when he met Alexandra. The thirty-year-old taxi driver had a wild side that appealed to Bernd. Alexandra went parachute training and tried to persuade Bernd to do it too. The couple went Rollerblading together. "You're the nicest, sweetest person I've ever met," Alexandra told Bernd. But their romance floundered after a few months. Something was missing, Alexandra felt. She didn't learn about Bernd's confused sexuality until after they had split up. "I'm bisexual," he told Alexandra. Later, when they remained friends, Bernd told her he was gay.

Bernd had decided that his preference was actually for men. He now focused on finding a male mate and exploring the gay side of his sexuality.

It wasn't long before he found a suitable partner.

Bernd met twenty-seven-year-old Rene Jasnik at a party. The two hit it off immediately and romance soon blossomed. Rene, a baker by trade, had dark hair and wore a ring in his left earlobe. He physically resembled Bernd's ex-girlfriend Bettina, with heavy thighs and a large lower body, which was set off by short, spiky hair and glasses. Rene shared the same interests as Bernd. He also liked surfing the Internet, and the two worked together to build up a PC network at home. Rene was at least ten years younger, and Bernd's quiet, conservative ways impressed him. Bernd gave him a sense of stability, unlike many other people that he had met in the gay scene. Bernd seemed respectable, somehow.

Rene became Bernd's long-term partner. The two men built up a happy, harmonious relationship, and at the end of 1999, Rene moved into Bernd's flat in Burchardstrasse, in the Berlin district of Tempelhof. They seemed a perfect pair, and it wasn't long before they started to behave like an old, married couple. They spent most evenings slumped in front of the television, with the occasional night out at the cinema; Rene was keen to avoid the more outlandish side of the gay scene. They had sex once or twice a week. Neither of them tried to incorporate torture or pain into their moments of intimacy.

Bernd kept his relationship with Rene secret from his colleagues. He still boasted at the office about his experiences with women, and his colleagues always presumed he was heterosexual. Bernd told his colleague Angela that a male friend lived with him in his apartment. But that didn't mean necessarily that he was gay, Angela thought.

Bernd now had a stable home life to complement his career as a successful, financially secure professional. After two years together, Bernd and Rene still seemed happy. Plans for the future inevitably unfolded. The couple started to think where they would spend their summer vacation.

Rene was thrilled when Siemens awarded Bernd a profit share of 15,000 marks. Bernd decided to invest it in their home and what Rene saw as their future together. They bought a new television set, a stereo, mobile phones, a fridge and a computer for the flat. Bernd also spent 899 marks on a silver mountain bike and decided to join a gym. Now that he had turned forty, he was desperate not to lose his sexual allure and started to work out obsessively.

Slim, dark-haired Bernd started boasting at work about his muscular body and claimed he had turned his paunch into a washboard stomach. He shaved all his hair off when he realized he was developing a bald patch. Angela, Stefan and his other colleagues nearly didn't recognize him when he came into a meeting the next morning.

Bernd was delighted.

He loved to provoke a reaction.

Bernd's colleagues—and Rene—had no idea of the inner turmoil raging inside him. Nor did they catch a glimpse of his sexual habits outside of his bedroom. Unknown to everyone he was close to, Bernd was spending more and more time with male prostitutes, whom he picked up outside Bahnhof Zoo, Berlin's main railway station.

Bernd had started to frequent prostitutes around this area after he split up with Ariane. By 1999, his dependence on the sexual services they provided had escalated; he went down to the station as many as three times *a day* to live out his fantasies with the hookers. With them, Bernd could give vent to his secret self; he could let himself be tortured to express his lack of self-worth and his desire to be humiliated.

Bernd developed favorites among the prostitutes.

One of them was tall, exotic-looking Immanuel, whom he chatted up in the fall of 1995. Immanuel was fit and Puerto Rican, with tight curly black hair and fashionable clothes. Bernd developed a friendship with him that went beyond the sexual pleasures he paid for. The two men enjoyed talking to each other and went out for walks, to the disco or to the cinema. Bernd started to make outrageous requests when he and Immanuel met, and demanded increasingly violent sex as their friendship progressed. He urged the rent boy to threaten to whip him. Immanuel agreed. Then Bernd started to urge Immanuel to whip him until he bled.

"I only want you to stop torturing me when the pain becomes unbearable," Bernd told the tall Puerto Rican.

Bernd's requests didn't ease up. He had opened the door to his innermost fantasies and unleashed a flood of uncontrollable sexual desires. His demands started to revolve around his lifelong desire to be castrated.

"Bite into my penis, bite it off!" he ordered Immanuel.

Immanuel played along and pretended to be a hungry cannibal who would pander to Bernd's needs; he was used to unusual requests by clients who had extreme fantasies. He didn't believe that Bernd really wanted to be mutilated.

Then one day, Bernd went a step farther and brought along a meat knife to one of their sessions.

"Chop it off—you can do with it what you will," he told Immanuel as he handed him the knife.

From then on, Bernd frequently begged Immanuel to cut off, bite off or eat his penis. The prostitute acted out various role-plays to keep Bernd happy, but he never dreamed of carrying out Bernd's requests. His view of Bernd shifted; he no longer saw him as a reserved man, but rather as an unhappy individual who was addicted to sex.

Cuban Victor Enrique also considered Bernd a nice man, albeit someone who had problems managing his sexual fantasies. Victor, thirty-eight, became another of Bernd's favorite prostitutes. Bernd also pressed Victor to amputate his penis with his teeth. Victor refused. Bernd, who was becoming more desperate, offered Victor 10,000 marks in December 2000 to bite off his male organ. Upon a further refusal from Victor, Bernd threw his car and his computer into the bargain if the prostitute would perform the act. Victor broke off contact with Bernd. He realized his client's desires were becoming pathological.

Bernd started to look further afield to fulfill his masochistic desires. The Internet seemed an obvious outlet. When Rene left for his job at the bakers at 1:30 A.M., Bernd would switch on his computer and visit torture Web sites. He logged on to cannibal chat rooms under the pseudonym "Cator," who was "born as flesh." Like Armin, he became a chat-room addict, and spent his nights meeting like-minded men in rooms such as the Cannibal Cafe, where they discussed their destructive tendencies and their desire for pain, humiliation and domination. He also started to post ads on the chat rooms to find someone to share his obscene fantasies with. "Looking for a manly man to help me leave this world," he wrote under his pseudonym.

In February 2001, Bernd saw Armin's ad requesting "people for slaughter." He read of Armin's hunt for a "young, well-built man who wants to be eaten." He replied. He offered himself to Armin, and insisted he was serious, though he lied in his e-mail about his age. He told Armin (or Franky) that he was six years younger than he was; he knew Armin was looking for a slaughter victim who was under thirty years old, and Bernd was forty-two.

The e-mail exchanges were frank and explicit. "I've wanted to be slaughtered and eaten ever since I was a child," Bernd confessed to Armin. And Armin admitted that his desire to eat someone had also started in childhood.

Bernd pored over the photos Armin had sent him of Armin's teeth.

"There's absolutely no way back for me, only forwards, through your teeth," Bernd declared. By now, he was prepared to do almost anything to fulfill his life's desire to tear off his unwanted penis, even if he had to sign a potential death pact to meet his wishes. It would be a type of annihilation, and the culmination of his self-worth conflict.

The bizarre pair began to make detailed arrangements to meet and act out their fantasies together.

9

I Hope
You'll
Find Me
Tasty

The morning of March 9, 2001, finally dawned. Bernd and
Armin both woke up to the realization that this day, so eagerly awaited, might change their lives forever.

Bernd felt strangely calm as he listened to the sounds of
the city waking up outside his bedroom window. Neighbors' cars were pulling out of their driveways as commuters set out for another day in the office. He turned over
in bed and looked at his partner, Rene, asleep beside him.
Rene didn't stir as Bernd gently moved back the bedclothes and got out of bed. The couple was used to getting
up at different times, as Rene worked early morning shifts
at the bakery, while Bernd followed a standard nine-to-five
routine. Bernd chose not to wake his partner; he didn't
want Rene to ask any questions or make any emotional
supplications that might change his mind. His mother had
disappeared from his life without saying goodbye, and
Bernd intended to follow her lead.

He moved quietly around the flat so as not to disturb Rene. He had a long shower, shaved carefully to avoid nicking his skin, and splashed himself with his favorite aftershave. Bernd looked at himself in the mirror. An attractive, healthy-looking man in his forties stared back, yet despite the luxurious apartment he lived in, the love of the man who lay in his bed and the responsibility of the job that he held, he still disgusted himself. Bernd got dressed in smart, casual clothes, his standard Friday office gear; a lot of Siemens employees wore slightly more relaxed attire on Fridays, in anticipation of the weekend ahead. Bernd wanted to look attractive, yet he didn't want to attract attention if he bumped into any neighbors or colleagues. He didn't want anyone to suspect that anything was out of the ordinary.

He ran through a mental checklist, to be sure that he didn't leave any clues as to his whereabouts. He had two concerns: he didn't want people to realize the depths he had sunk to in order to be castrated and annihilated, and he wanted to play for time. He didn't know how long it would take before Armin would slaughter him. He didn't want anyone to track him down in the meantime. So he switched on his computer and erased all his files. He cleared his Internet history to conceal his frequent visits to cannibal and torture Web sites, and he wiped the computer hard drive clean to remove all of his e-mail exchanges with Armin. A month of written confessions of cravings for flesh, and detailed plans of how to satisfy them, disappeared with a few clicks of a mouse. Bernd then read through a copy of his will and looked around for a place to hide it. He didn't want Rene to stumble across the legal document immediately. Bernd had made the will out a few days earlier, and had it officially certified by a notary. He had left the bulk of his estate to his live-in partner. Rene would inherit Bernd's lavish penthouse apartment and his collection of computer equipment, worth about $50,000. Bernd had sold most of his other belongings, including his sports car, for several thousand euros. He put the cash and his passport in his back pocket. If necessary, he could pay Armin to persuade him to amputate his penis. His passport would provide a proof of identity to his would-be mutilator.

Bernd cast one last glance at Rene, who was still sleeping peacefully, and left.

Rene awoke in an empty bed, looking forward to the weekend ahead and some quiet time with Bernd. He got up and walked through to the kitchen to make some breakfast. Bernd hadn't mentioned any particular meetings that day, so Rene hoped he would be home on time. Maybe they could go to the cinema that evening, he thought. He had no idea that Bernd planned to leave both him and this world today. Rene did not realize his live-in lover had thoughts of suicide, or any appetite for destruction. As far as he was concerned, his lover had left for a normal day at the office.

But Bernd wasn't on the way to the office. He had informed his employers that he needed a day's leave to "attend to some personal matters." He told his colleagues he was going to fly to London to see a specialist about his hair loss. His colleagues didn't question his motives. They were familiar with Bernd's vanity and his increasing preoccupation with his looks.

Bernd's real journey that morning took him back to Bahnhof Zoo. He knew the route well from his regular visits to prostitutes in the area, though this time he avoided talking to the hookers who loitered on the streets outside Berlin's main train station. He was through with role-plays of domination and pain. This time, he wanted the real thing. He wanted the opportunity to fulfill a lifelong dream.

Bernd bought a one-way ticket to Kassel, where he had arranged to meet Armin.

He paid for his ticket in cash so nobody could trace his journey.

As he waited for his train, he ignored his gnawing stomach pains and suppressed the desire to eat any of the croissants or sandwiches that were on display at the various snack stands scattered around the station. He deliberately didn't want to eat anything, so that his intestines remained empty. According to cannibal Web sites, this would make the slaughter easier and his meat tastier.

The train arrived and Bernd boarded and looked around for a seat. It was an ICE train, one of the modern trains that link up Germany's high-speed train network. It would take just under three hours to travel the three hundred kilometers from Berlin to Kassel Wilhelmshöhe. Bernd had to change trains once in Hanover to reach his destination.

Bernd reclined on the blue, patterned train seat and tried to relax. He rested his head against the seat's gray cushion as the train pulled out of the station and the world started to speed past his window. He felt dizzy and weak from a lack of food. His temples contracted as a throbbing headache started to spread across his forehead. His body seemed strangely light and he felt removed from reality. The train stewardess wheeled her trolley past, offering passengers "Coffee, snacks or soft drinks." Bernd ignored her offer, and shut his eyes for a few minutes to try and focus. The train was almost empty. Few passengers were traveling to Kassel at such an early hour. The small number of people who sat in his carriage seemed set for a long weekend visiting relatives.

Bernd stared at the old woman sitting opposite him. She

was surrounded by newspapers and food, which she had bought to occupy herself during the journey to her daughter and grandchildren's house. *I'm not going to grow that old, if today goes as planned,* Bernd likely thought to himself. *I'm still going to be fit and healthy when I die. At least I won't have to watch myself turn into an old man, whose body has gone to pieces and who can't do anything without asking for help. This way I'll have control of how and when I die.*

The old woman felt someone's eyes on her and glanced at her neighbor, who was staring at her with a distant expression on his face. She adjusted her glasses and returned to her newspaper crossword. She didn't suspect that, one day, the same regional newspaper would be filled with photos and headlines about the unassuming man opposite her.

A young female conductor, with her hair in a bun and wearing a neatly ironed white blouse and blue trouser suit, walked into the carriage. She checked the passengers' tickets as she walked through the train compartment. She smiled at Bernd as he gave her his ticket to punch and validate. "Do you just want a one-way ticket to Kassel or do you need to buy a return?" she asked.

"No, just one-way, please," Bernd replied. "I'm not sure if I'm coming back."

Who knows what Bernd pondered during this ride? Perhaps he cast his mind back over his life, and thought about the strained relationship he had with his father and the vague, patchwork memories he had of his mother and his early childhood? Perhaps he thought about all the people he had cared about in his life and would leave behind. Ariane, his long-term girlfriend, and now Rene, who no doubt would be pottering around the apartment getting ready for work? They were probably all better off without him, he may have thought to himself.

Bernd remained determined to carry out his plan. He

felt an overwhelming need to be castrated. His sexuality disgusted him; his life and body would be extinguished if he were eaten, and he didn't want his corpse to rot away in the ground or his ashes to sit on someone's mantelpiece. He wanted to *totally* disappear. He was able to feel a sense of reverse domination at the thought of being consumed. He knew how much Armin wanted to eat him, and that gave him a sense of power.

He had something that Armin *wanted*.

That fateful morning, Armin had woken up early and eaten a light breakfast. He had also taken a day off work, and was busy at home preparing for his "slaughter boy."

Adrenaline pumped through Armin's body as he started up his car and drove to the shops. He bought enough groceries for two, including potatoes, brussels sprouts, garlic, Italian porcini mushrooms and freshly ground coffee. He also bought some candles to add a more intimate atmosphere to the house and the dinner table. He lingered over the store's collection of red wine, and finally settled on a South African red, a wine the color of blood.

Armin drove home and started to clean the kitchen and living room. He glanced around the slaughter room to see if everything was in place. He dusted the makeshift butcher's table and polished his kitchen knives. He ran his finger along the blades to check they were sharp enough and then arranged them on the table. He hoped that Bernd would like the homemade abattoir, with its meat hooks and troughs, as much as he did. He toyed with the mannequins hung by a nail on the wall. Maybe he could hang Bernd's head there? At last, he would have a real human to dissect and devour! He wouldn't have to play make-believe anymore.

Armin switched on his computer downstairs and reread

some of the fantasies and e-mails he had exchanged with
Bernd. "Whoever REALLY wants to do it, needs a REAL
VICTIM!" Bernd had written under the name of Cator.
Worry began to wash over Armin. Would Bernd really go
through with it? He *seemed* to be a genuine slaughter victim. But what if he didn't turn up at the station? Armin had
been let down in the past by people who had promised to
meet him and then backed out at the last minute. . . .

Armin breathed deeply to calm his nerves.

Then he got in his car and drove to Kassel train station.

There were two main stations in Kassel; Armin drove to
the new ICE Bahnhof Wilhelmshöhe station, which was
three kilometers west of the city center. This station was a
major ICE transfer point, which brought money and business to the reconstructed town on the Fulda River, which
lay about ninety minutes north of Frankfurt, Germany's, financial center. He waited on the platform for the white ICE
train to pull into the station. He checked his watch. The
train was on time. He watched the passengers disembark.
They were laden with suitcases as they kissed their loved
ones who were waiting for them. Bernd's figure finally
emerged from behind a group of people who were getting
off near the back of the train. Armin waved at Bernd, who
smiled back and walked over to him.

Recognition was easy; they had poured over photos of
each other naked.

Armin stared at the dark-haired, athletic man in front of
him. He was better looking than his photo! He struggled to
find the right words. Bernd, meanwhile, ran his eyes over
the gaunt, bespectacled man in front of him. "I am your
Cator. I am your flesh," he said. "I hope you'll find me
tasty."

10

The
Slaughter
Room

Armin felt a sense of relief; Bernd hadn't changed his mind. The two men walked along the platform and up a slope to the station's main hall. They felt at ease with each other, and had both acknowledged before they met that they felt they'd found their potential twin, their polar oppo site who could complete their respective needs. Armin found Bernd attractive, even though he wasn't "his type," namely tall and blond. He was impressed by Bernd's fit physique. Bernd felt glad that Armin appeared to be a gentleman, and was someone he could relate to on a friendly basis as well on an erotic level. They passed an instant photo booth, and a stall that sold freshly baked bread rolls. The stall was plastered with signs reading "Frankie's Brezelpoint" and promised its goods tasted "delicious."

"I hope that Franky will find me just as delicious," Bernd joked. Then he asked Armin, "Have you got any painkillers or sleeping tablets at home? I'm going to need enough drugs to knock me out cold to block the pain. I don't want to feel anything during the slaughter. I want to slip away, without suffering."

"I've got some pills at home, but probably not enough," Armin replied. "But there's a drugstore around the corner. Let's get some more, just in case.

"I've got a bottle of Wicks MediNait medicine at home," Armin continued. "You know, the stuff you take to help you sleep when you've got a cough or a cold. It's got alcohol in it, I think. And how about a bottle of something maybe? That should do the trick. Which do you prefer, brandy or Schnapps?"

"Let's buy some Schnapps," said Bernd. "It's probably stronger and anyhow, I prefer the taste."

"I think we're all right for food," Armin said. "But is there anything in particular you fancy? I mean we could pick something up now, if you like."

"Not for me, thanks," Bernd said. "I haven't eaten anything for the last two days, so my stomach should be empty. And I want to keep it that way. You know, it's meant to make me taste better."

"Well, I should be okay, anyway, then," Armin joked. "Hopefully, I'm taking you home for dinner. You're certainly giving me an appetite." He gazed appreciatively at his companion's body.

Bernd took the compliment well. "It'll be the best meal you've ever had, hopefully," he smiled.

"Oh, I'm absolutely sure about that," Armin said. "I've been hungry for you for a long time."

The men made their way to the station pharmacy, Ihr Platz Express. The drugstore offered groceries, sweets and everything you could need for a journey, from chocolate to magazines, as well as medicine. They bought a packet of sleeping tablets and a large bottle of Schnapps. The clear German liquor has a high alcohol content and is guaranteed to intoxicate, or in Bernd's case, help render him unconscious.

They carried their purchases past the huddle of bikes parked outside the station. Once they were outside, trams trundled past them, transporting Kassel citizens about their daily business. They headed toward Armin's car, which was parked in the station car park. Armin loaded the trunk with their shopping and opened the passenger door for Bernd.

When he got inside the car, Bernd felt his energy levels plummet once more, just as they had on the train. He found it difficult to concentrate as a fog enveloped his thought processes, and his limbs became heavy. His body was reacting to its lack of food. His eyesight was slightly blurred, and reality seemed to fade away as Armin pointed out Kassel landmarks to him. He shut his eyes for a minute to collect his strength, then fixed his attention on the scenery around him.

The streets of Kassel were busy with shoppers and businessmen; as they traveled out of the city center and into suburbia, they were surrounded by rows of apartment blocks and detached houses. Mothers watched over their children, who were playing on the swings and roundabouts in the numerous suburban parks. Then they reached the countryside. Wide fields on either side of the road opened out into gentle, sloping hills, scattered with trees. A river fed the agricultural expanse, and a few half-timbered farmhouses, as well as sheep and cows, populated the otherwise deserted area.

Bernd felt more alert as he opened the car window and let the fresh air of a beautiful spring day blow in on his face. He looked over at Armin. "So, this is it at last," he said.

"Yes," Armin replied. "You know I've been waiting for this day for a long time. I almost thought it would never happen. I mean, I've wanted to find someone like you for so long. Someone who was really serious about cannibalism and not just pretending, like the other people I've met. You do really want to go through with it? You really want me to eat you?"

Bernd smiled. "You know I wouldn't be here if I didn't, would I? I told you in my e-mails how much I want all of this."

"Oh, you don't know how good that is to hear," Armin said. "I was worried that you wouldn't want to go through with it after all."

"There's no need to worry," Bernd reassured him. "So you haven't done this before then?"

"No, but I've always wanted to," Armin replied. "I feel that this is what I was born to do. Somehow, it's my life's purpose."

"I can't wait for you to castrate me," Bernd said longingly. "Just the thought of it excites me so much. You've no idea how much I want to get rid of my penis. I can't wait for you to bite it off!"

"And I can't wait to taste your flesh in my mouth," Armin said, looking over at his passenger. "I don't know which piece to eat first. I just want to eat you all up. There's those taut thighs of yours for a start."

"Oh, my penis, it has to be my penis first," Bernd said. "That's what I really want."

"Well, you know, as with most of the animal kingdom, castration ensures a tender filet," Armin teased. "I really can't wait."

"You shouldn't have to wait too long. I want to do it as soon as possible. Today, ideally. Not next week or anything."

"I'm glad you're so eager," Armin said. "I've got everything ready. The knives and all the equipment. The table should be the perfect height and width to work on your body. I think you're going to like the slaughter room."

"Oh, I'm sure I will," Bernd replied. "And I've cleared my computer's hard drive like you told me and taken a day off work. No one should have any idea that I'm here. Hopefully no one ever will and I'll just vanish out of existence."

"I don't see why they should find anything out, as long as we're careful," Armin said.

"It's great to think that I won't have to die alone or suffer some painful death rotting away in a nursing home," Bernd said. "I don't want my body to waste away in the ground or end up as worm food."

"No, this way you'll have a nice death," Armin said. "We'll fulfill our mutual purposes. You'll disappear and I'll have your meat and won't be alone anymore. I'll have you with me always. You can become a part of me."

The two started to discuss the details of the slaughter, and a plan took shape. Bernd would take a cocktail of sleeping pills and Armin's cough medicine. The mixture would serve as an anesthetic to stun the pain from the first thrusts of Armin's knife. Bernd wanted Armin to consume everything edible on his body, and Armin agreed. He had learned about all the possible cuts of meat that lay beneath a man's skin and was more than willing to consume all of them. He would dispose of the innards and leftovers from Bernd's carcass, he promised. He also told Bernd of his plan to film the killing using his video camera. That way, he could relive the whole slaughter scene afterward and remember the pleasure.

"But tell me why you want to do it," Armin said. "I want to make sure you're ready to go through with all of this."

"Oh, I am," Bernd replied. "I want to destroy myself. To disappear from the face of the planet. I hate myself so much. I despise my sexuality and the way I want sex all the time. I'm just a worthless piece of meat and bones. There's no place left for me in this world. I've had it."

"Well, I want you," Armin said. "I think you're the most precious thing that has walked into my life since my mother and my brother. You're the brother I always wanted. You're the person I want to make me whole. I don't think you're worthless at all. In fact, quite the opposite."

The hills flattened out again as they approached Armin's home. Bernd and Armin drove through the forested area on the outskirts of Rotenburg and arrived at Wüstefeld. The journey had taken an hour. The two men had resolved a lot during those sixty minutes. They were both now certain that the words sent by e-mail were not just playful, sexual taunts but the expression of each other's innermost needs. Bernd looked around at Armin's home village. "I more or less grew up here," Armin said proudly.

The cluster of houses and the peaceful countryside backdrop seemed a million miles away from the roar of traffic, the pollution and the hordes of people Bernd had left behind that morning in Berlin. It was a rare, quiet place in a busy world. It seemed the perfect place to disappear from. Armin gave his guest a quick synopsis of who lived in the houses around his home. There was the nationalist, who had painted slogans on the walls of his house in bright, garish colors. And then there was the businessman who'd made the headlines of the local newspapers after being accused of swindling people. Slightly up the hill, behind Armin's house, was the Schnaars' farm, where Armin bought his eggs at the weekend. And next door to Armin's place was the house where Ulla von Bernus, the famous satanic priestess, used to live. Armin quickly summarized the story of his mother's former best friend, and her capacity to summon unwanted husbands and wives to their deaths.

A new couple, Hartmut and Daniella Schroeder, had moved into Ulla's farmhouse now. Armin had yet to get to know them; they had erected fierce "Keep Out" signs on either side of the gate leading into their drive.

And that left Armin's house. The sun shone down on the sprawling manor in front of them. Armin opened the gate, drove along his gravel driveway and parked his car alongside his collection of old vehicles. The heaps of metal would look better off in a scrap yard, Bernd thought, but he kept quiet. "Well, here we are then," he said.

The two men stalled outside, by the car. Armin suddenly felt awkward and unsure of what to do and say next.

"I can't believe that you live here all by yourself," Bernd said, breaking the silence. "I mean it's massive. How many rooms are there?"

"Oh, at least thirty," Armin replied. "Of course, I used to live here with Mother, until she passed away. I don't know if I'll ever get over her death."

"Aren't you tempted to sell it or do something with it?" Bernd asked.

"Well, I've often thought about turning it into a hotel or a residential center where people could come and take computer courses. Of course, it needs a bit of work done to it. And then there's the whole money aspect. It costs a lot to do up a place like this."

"Yes, sure, I appreciate that," Bernd replied. "It just seems such a shame to let it all go to waste."

"Well, maybe someday I'll get around to it," Armin said. "I'm beginning to believe that dreams really can come true. All this feels like a dream, standing here with you, outside my home."

"Yeah, tell me about it," Bernd said. "So what happens next in your dream?"

Armin paused for a moment. "To be honest, it never started out here by the car. When I fantasize about this type of thing, which is a lot, I'm already inside the house and so is the man I'm going to eat."

"Well, I guess we'd better go in then and start the dream sequence," Bernd said.

Armin led his dinner guest up the steps to his front door and into his entrance hall. He took Bernd's jacket, and Bernd felt as if he had stepped back in time. He walked through a hall and up the stairs into a living room that housed age-old furniture, musty carpets and wall hangings. "I've never seen anything like this place," he said. "It looks as if no one has lived here for centuries. I mean, everything's so old-fashioned."

"Well, Mother liked it this way and I didn't want to change it after she died," Armin said defensively.

"I guess I'm just used to living in a modern apartment," Bernd said quickly, not wishing to offend his new friend. "It's certainly different, that's for sure."

Armin showed Bernd around the rest of the ground floor. There was the lounge where he relaxed in the evenings, which adjoined the room where he worked on his computers and accessed the electronic world of cannibal Web sites. He showed Bernd the computer he used to log on to the Internet and send his e-mails, where he'd sat and fantasized about this very moment. Then he showed his guest the summer house and the extension that overlooked the road. Bernd murmured polite noises in response to the tour. Armin could see that his guest was tired. "Do you want a coffee?" he asked. "Or maybe something stronger?"

Bernd settled on a coffee.

He needed a caffeine fix to sharpen his senses for the games ahead.

11

You Have My Word and My Permission to Kill Me

Armin hurried into the kitchen to prepare some coffee to revive his guest. He stood on a stool to reach an overhead cupboard, where his mother had stacked her best crockery, and blew the dust off some of the floral-patterned cups and saucers. He had seldom used the delicate china cups since his mother's death. His parents had been given the rose-and-white-colored dinner service as a wedding present and his mother had instructed Armin to save the best china for "special occasions" or an "important meal." It normally only graced the dinner table at Christmas or on birthdays.

Armin carefully placed a teaspoon at the correct angle on each saucer and arranged the cups on the top left-hand side of the tea tray, just as his mother had taught him. Waltraud would have been pleased to see that her lessons in good conduct had made a lasting impression. But she never would have dreamed that her youngest son would hope to serve human flesh from her precious dinner service. She may have taught him the correct way to lay the table and hold his china cup—but she didn't show him how to function socially. Armin's lust for flesh wasn't entirely his mother's fault; but had she behaved differently during his formative years, and allowed him to grow in independence and character, his perversion might never have reared its ugly head. The rigorous parameters she set denied her son the world of girls, dating and stolen kisses. Armin's sexuality had, instead, been deformed during its nascent years. Just as other people became obsessed with high heels or rubber dresses, Armin's fetish was for a man's meat. It was the handling of human flesh that was the source of his sexual satisfaction. But he was still a virgin in terms of cannibalism. Tonight might change that, he thought excitedly.

His heart was pounding in his chest and his hands were trembling as he set a china milk jug on the tray and poured boiling water over the coffee. He breathed in the strong aroma of the freshly ground beans and tried to relax as he waited for the coffee to brew. It all seemed too good to be true, the stuff of dreams. Sitting in his house, just in the other room, was a man who was willing to be sacrificed for him! Here was someone who was prepared to take on the role of his long-lost brother, to always reside in him. Here, at last, was a like-minded man who was happy to die for his longed-for rebirth!

Armin filled up a jug with water that had been chilling in the fridge and added it and two glasses to his laden tray. He wanted to make sure that Bernd didn't dehydrate from drinking too much coffee. Bernd needed to drink plenty of water to help flush out his system after his fast, to purge any stored toxins and bodily wastes, and make bleeding easier.

Armin took the tray through to his guest.

"Well, aren't you the good host," Bernd said in a flirtatious tone.

Armin stopped in the doorway and stared at his guest, who was sitting in a wicker chair by the coffee table. Bernd was completely naked but for his glasses. His clothes lay in an abandoned heap on the floor besides him.

Armin put down the tray on the coffee table and ran his eyes over his guest's body. Bernd was toned and muscular. He was a little overweight, yet still in excellent shape. Bernd's photo hadn't done him justice, Armin thought. Here was an attractive man in his prime. A fine fillet of meat. He let his gaze fall on Bernd's muscular neck and shoulders. Bernd had strong arms and masculine hands. The corners of Armin's mouth curled up into an appreciative smile. Bernd's eyes sparkled back with mischief.

"Now you can see my body," he said, standing.

"Oh, you look absolutely delicious," Armin said. "What a sight!"

Armin took two steps toward his guest; Bernd held his gaze. Suddenly Armin's breath was on Bernd's forehead, and his arms were draped around his shoulders. Bernd closed his eyes, his arms hanging limp at his sides, as the two stood there in silence. Bernd felt he could hardly breathe as Armin brushed his lips across his forehead, settling on each eyelid softly. Bernd responded by wrapping his arms around his host. The two stayed there a few minutes, taking in each other's smell and the touch of skin.

"It's going to be okay, isn't it?" Bernd asked softly.

"Of course," Armin answered. "We've found each other now, that's the important thing. It's all going to be all right."

They broke their embrace and smiled at each other.

"Let me undress you," Bernd said. "You're wearing far too many clothes for my liking."

Bernd unbuttoned Armin's shirt, pulled it free of Armin's trousers and slipped it off his shoulders. He unlaced his shoes and took them off along with his socks. Then he unbuckled Armin's belt and pulled down his trousers. Armin stood in front of him naked. "Come on, let's drink our coffee before it goes cold," Bernd said. "We may need it later. I guess we've got a long night ahead of us."

The two men sat down, pulled their chairs close to the table and drank their afternoon coffee naked, bathing in the sunlight that poured through the windows.

"I've never done this before in this room", Armin said.

"Oh, it's much more fun without clothes," Bernd replied. "Though I guess you have to watch out you don't spill any hot coffee in your lap!"

Armin laughed and gazed across the table at Bernd. "You've no idea how much I've wanted to see someone like you sitting there," he said. "But I still want to be one hundred percent sure. Are you certain you want to go ahead with this? It's not too late to change your mind. I only want someone who's completely willing to be eaten."

"Look, you have my word and my permission to kill me, if that's what you need," Bernd said. "I'm your Cator, your flesh, remember."

Armin was overjoyed; his victim's consent played an integral role in his fantasy. He didn't want to eat someone against his will. Devouring a dead body pulled from a grave, or dragged from the scene of an accident, wouldn't have given him the same thrill. He needed someone who would agree to become his little brother inside of him; unlike most adults, who abandoned their fantasy friends when they grew out of their toys, Armin still carried Franky, his fantasy friend, around with him. He now wanted to combine reality with fantasy. Bernd would become a real blood brother to live inside him.

The two men exchanged cannibal tidbits over their coffee.

In many countries, the consumption of flesh wasn't considered a crime, Armin told Bernd. He had seen a news report where starving North Koreans resorted to cannibalism for sustenance after going insane with hunger in 1997. They even killed and ate their own infants. And the Tartar hordes who swept over Europe in 1242 were particularly fond of young girls, he said. Appetizing young maidens were issued as rations to army officers, while common soldiers chewed on the tough flesh of older women. Breast meat was regarded as the finest tidbit and was reserved for the prince's table. And the Fore people of Papua New Guinea traditionally ate their dead at mortuary feasts. "I just wish cannibalism were allowed in Germany too," Armin said longingly. "I really can't understand why it isn't."

Bernd nodded in agreement. "Did you read about the young factory worker in Uganda who said in court that he was proud to be a cannibal, after being arrested for trespassing on a burial site?" he asked. The young Ugandan dug up corpses and ate them, after they had been buried, as he didn't like to see the meat go to waste. He waited at least a week after the funeral, out of respect to the relatives and because the meat tasted better once it had matured, Bernd informed Armin.

Bernd related more of his favorite cannibal anecdotes, which he had gathered from cannibal Web sites, as Armin poured out more coffee.

During World War I, the British minister of food, Lord Woolton, carefully considered but finally rejected a plan, proposed by his government scientists, to feed the country on black pudding made from surplus human blood bank donations, Bernd told Armin.

His favorite cannibal tale took place in the U.S. He narrated to Armin how in 1977, U.S. government officials staged a grand opening ceremony of their new Department of Agriculture staff canteen, attended by Robert Bergland, U.S. agriculture secretary. Bergland unveiled a brass plaque, naming it the "Alfred Packer Memorial Dining Facility," after one of America's most famous nineteenth-century frontiersmen. A few months later the plaque was hurriedly removed when someone remembered what the late Mr. Packer had been chiefly famous for: he was a cannibal convicted of killing and eating five Colorado gold prospectors in the 1870s.

"Oh, I know a good story," Armin replied. "I read about it the other day on the Internet." He told the tale of when Stanley Dean Baker was stopped in Monterey County, California, for possible involvement in a hit-and-run accident. Baker shocked the arresting officer when he uttered the phrase "I have a problem, I'm a cannibal." To prove his point, he pulled a handful of human fingers out of his pocket. The fingers, which Baker had been snacking on, belonged to the hand of a missing twenty-two-year-old social worker named James Schlosser. Baker, who wasn't a shy cannibal, boasted to police about eating Schlosser's heart raw, and claimed to have developed a taste for human flesh while undergoing electroshock therapy for a nervous disorder.

The two men laughed. They understood what had driven the criminals to cannibalism, even if they accepted that most of the world didn't.

"So what about me and you?" Bernd asked. "I can see you want me. How shall I make my grand finale? My final exit?"

Armin knew that under ideal conditions, his victim should be stunned into insensitivity. Sharp blows to the head were best. If not, a single bullet through the middle of the forehead or back of the skull could suffice. But he knew he couldn't do that to Bernd. He didn't want to use unnecessary violence, nor did he have a gun. He also didn't want to excite Bernd or cause a struggle, as this would pump a greater volume of blood and secretions—such as adrenaline—through the body. He reached for Bernd's shoulders and pulled his friend toward him so that they were staring directly into each other's eyes.

"I want to stab you to death, gut you and carve you up," Armin whispered. "Then I'll eat you."

Armin also planned to saw through one or both of Bernd's legs at the points directly below the groin and a few inches above the knee. Once skinned, these portions could be cut into round steaks of his preferred thickness, then into fillets, and deboned for a roast or a hearty steak, he told his friend.

He wanted to avoid the use of human fat and intestines in his recipes. "I've never been an experimental chef," he joked to Bernd.

The evening sun sank behind the old manor house as two men chattered away, absorbed in their plans.

"Let's go upstairs and I'll show you the slaughter room," Armin said.

He swung open the door of Bernd's future funeral parlor and watched his friend's face. Bernd's reaction was everything he had hoped for.

"But this is incredible!" Bernd exclaimed as he walked inside. Bernd fingered the meat hooks where Armin planned to hang his carcass. He examined the large table where he would lie, the tub for waste trimmings from his body and the hose to wash away his blood.

Armin set up his home video camera to film the human butchering. He pressed the record button and soon images of two naked men caressing each other and joking were recorded.

Bernd and Armin guessed the shapes of the animals that were formed by the shadows dancing on the rust-stained walls. They lost themselves to make-believe for a few minutes, like children who stare at the clouds in the sky.

"Do you see the ibex there?" asked Bernd.

"Or is it a donkey?" Armin laughed.

The dungeonlike cell measured three meters by four meters wide and was devoid of windows or natural light. The only light was a stark glare emanating from neon tubes on the ceiling. The room smelled of mildew and decay, like the rest of the centuries-old house. For the two men, though, it seemed the perfect setting for their lovemaking.

Music played quietly from the portable radio in the room as Bernd sank into Armin's embrace. Armin stroked his arms and ran his hands gently over his throat and cheeks.

"You have nothing to worry about," Armin whispered.

He learned the weight of Bernd's thighs, the touch of his fingers, the heat of his breath and the curl of his tongue as they lay in the rusty cell for hours, wrapped up in an embrace, having sex or smoking cigarettes. They had found each other at last. Now they were ready to form a deeper union of flesh.

12

To Test
the Limits
of Pain

Bernd stirred, broke free of Armin's embrace and sat up on the bed.

He pulled back the blankets, which, after not being aired for so long in the damp house, smelled like rotten vegetables. He looked at Armin, who was lying still, dreaming, drugged from so much touching. He stroked the side of Armin's face, moved toward him and offered his mouth. The men kissed and their breath mingled. Sex had been pleasant, but the threads that bound the two of them were of a more violent, destructive nature. Erotic images formed in Bernd's mind: he pictured Armin biting into his penis and ripping the shreds of flesh free of his body. He imagined how Armin would use his teeth to tear off his sexual organ so completely that nothing remained, not even a stump. He felt passionate again. His blood was in a state of fire and he wanted to be burned. "Don't you think it's time to take things a bit further? To test the limits of pain and break through them?" he asked quietly.

Armin looked over at his new lover, and smiled.

After years of retreating into his violent imagination instead of forming relationships with others, his fantasies were spilling out into reality. He was about to act out his blood-drenched dreams. "You're right, we've waited long enough," he said. "It's time to start the pain! I want to devour your flesh for you to become alive in me."

Bernd stared directly into Armin's eyes. "I want an appetizer for the feast ahead," he said boldly. "I want you to bite me. I want you to bite my penis so hard that you draw blood! And then as you swallow my blood, I want you to start to chew and bite the whole thing off!" Bernd became more and more aroused; he closed his eyes and pictured blood gushing from his member. His sex was erect as he opened his eyes and saw Armin draw near.

Armin steadied his hand on Bernd's shoulder and knelt in front of him. He looked up at Bernd for guidance. Unlike his cannibalistic fantasies, which he cherished and planned in detail, castration wasn't something he'd ever imagined. This was *Bernd's* personal turn-on, not his.

"Bite into it! Please. Just bite it. Hard!" Bernd urged. He was convulsed with excitement as he looked down and saw Armin's teeth about to bite into his penis. He was trembling from head to foot. His eyes were dilated and his nerves were set for a climax, tense, responsive.

Armin opened his mouth wider. His lips were retracted and his gums were exposed like those of a wild beast, growling before his prey. He prepared to puncture Bernd's skin and drive his teeth into his flesh.

Bernd was hypnotized as he watched Armin's mouth close in on his penis. He felt as if electricity was pulsating through his veins as his excitement grew. "Do it! Bite me! Sink your teeth into me. Come *on!*"

But at the crucial moment, Armin hesitated and pulled back. He couldn't bring himself to bite into Bernd.

"No! You have to do it! Damn it, you can't stop now! *Bite it!*" Bernd screamed.

He grabbed Armin's hair and pushed his head down toward his sex.

Armin told himself that this was a necessary evil. He had to fulfill this request to get his meat. He took a deep breath and tightly clenched his right-hand fist. His teeth slowly enclosed Bernd's sexual organ and he felt the rapid pulse of blood. He wondered how it would taste.

Bernd was beside himself. "Yes, that's right! Now! *Go on!*"

Armin shut his eyes, gripped the flesh and slowly pressed his teeth in harder. He increased the pressure until his teeth met with the resistance of muscle. He stopped, opened his mouth slightly and tried again. This time, he actually bit Bernd, albeit gently.

"That's it. That's good. Now harder!" Bernd's voice grew rasping as he felt Armin's tongue around his most sensitive organ and imagined him swallowing his penis forever.

Armin got into position again. But try as he might, he couldn't bite Bernd hard enough; he couldn't go through with it.

Bernd felt the full cruelty of a lost opportunity. He was numb, his body felt dead, as he experienced the bitterness of disappointment and defeat. He pulled away. "It's not going to happen, is it?" he said finally.

Armin was too ashamed to talk. He had seen the potency of Bernd's desire. He could taste how much Bernd wanted it.

"You're too nice, too weak," Bernd said, as tinges of contempt entered his voice. "You're not tough enough to carry it through. I should have realized it earlier."

Bernd sank back on the mattress and hugged himself as he rocked slightly from side to side. He couldn't believe that he had been so close, and had lost. He suddenly felt exhausted. He didn't have the energy to talk or get up. He just wanted to lie there, lifeless, and forget about everything for a few minutes. He so badly wanted to be mutilated. He felt so helpless. He was so unhappy with his life and the prospect of staying alive. Surely the chance to die wouldn't be taken away from him too. This was the way he wanted to die! He had locked away his innermost fantasies and kept them a secret; he had led a double life, keeping his self-destructive tendencies hidden from Rene and his earlier partners. But he had exposed himself completely to Armin. And now he wasn't prepared to accept that it had all been in vain.

"What are you thinking?" Armin asked, as worry made his voice tremble. He was starting to panic. He didn't want to castrate Bernd, but he was still desperate to kill and eat him.

"I just want to feel my penis being mutilated," Bernd replied quietly. "I want to watch you devour me piece by piece. That's it, really."

"And I can't wait to become one with you, for you to become a part of me," Armin reassured him. "You're going to taste exquisite! There's no need to worry or stop now."

Bernd felt his insides warm with fresh hope. Maybe there was a chance? Maybe all wasn't lost after all. "What I really want, Armin, is for you to castrate me while I'm fully conscious," he said. "I want to watch you eat me alive." He took a deep breath and chose his words carefully before continuing. He didn't want his new plan to backfire. "But I'm not sure that you're up to that. You're far too good-natured. I think it would be easier for you if I were asleep. Then you can castrate me without witnessing my pain. What do you think?"

"Oh, I think that sounds like a brilliant plan," Armin said, desperate to seize any thread of opportunity. He felt relief flood his body. "Don't worry, this is going to work."

Armin ran down the stairs to the bathroom. He fetched his bottle of Wicks MediNait from the bathroom cabinet, the cough and cold mixture that makes patients drowsy. *This should put Bernd to sleep,* he thought. He hurried back to the slaughter room and presented him with the bottle, like a child with a gift. He was pleased that they had found a solution that would enable him to still have Bernd for dinner. Bernd glanced briefly at the ingredients listed on the label, then knocked back the contents of the bottle in one shot.

The two men looked at each other, as if they expected the medicine to immediately take effect. They laughed, realizing each other's thoughts. Half an hour passed, and Bernd still didn't feel at all tired. MediNait (known elsewhere as Night Nurse) has a relatively high alcohol content, but the excitement of the prospective amputation triumphed over the medicine's sedative effects. An hour passed and Bernd's limbs still didn't grow heavy, nor did his mind become cloudy. Indeed, he continued to feel fully awake and remained as alert as ever. Armin checked his pulse. It hadn't slowed. Each man recognized the other's frustration. How could their plan fail at the last hurdle?

"It's not working," Bernd said eventually. "It's not going to happen."

Bernd was no longer sure Armin was the right man for the job of human butcher—he doubted Armin was brutal enough to kill and eat him. It had all gone wrong, he concluded sadly. "I want to go home," he said. "Take me back to the station, please. I want to go back to Berlin."

Armin saw paradise slip out of his grasp.

His longed-for brother, his wished for soul mate was going to abandon him too, just like his mother, his brothers

and his father had done before him. He should have known
better, he thought, as disappointment crushed his insides.
He switched off his video camera. The men dressed and
left the slaughter room. It took their eyes a while to adjust
to the light in the rest of the house after the hours inhabited
in their dark cell. They dressed, left the house and got back
into Armin's car. They had been so hopeful the last time
they had sat there. But the atmosphere between them now
was flat, their optimism punctured.

Armin started up the car, headed out of the driveway and
started the hour-long journey back to Kassel train station.

Armin was silent as he drove and struggled with his
thoughts. He didn't want to let his cherished dream slip
through his fingers. He still wanted to attain the sexual satisfaction to be had from Bernd's flesh and blood. He made
up his mind. He would persuade Bernd that the soft hands
on the car's steering wheel were more than capable of de-
livering mortal blows.

"You know, Bernd, from the first moment I saw you, I
wondered which part of you I should eat first. All I know is
that I want to eat all of you. I can imagine what your flesh
is like. Glistening red meat that looks a little like tender
beef. I know it would melt in my mouth. Nothing would be
more delicious."

Bernd didn't say anything as he listened to Armin's se-
ductive tones.

"Have you any idea how much the idea of ripping apart
your fit, young body turns me on?" Armin continued. "I
have this amazing erotic image in my head of thrusting a
knife into you and watching you die. I want to witness your
blood, agony and death at first hand."

Armin knew the words that Bernd wanted to hear.

But Bernd was still uncertain of Armin's resolve.

"I know you say that now, Armin," he said in his quiet manner. "But in reality, could you carry it off? I'm really not so sure."

"Of course I'm able to kill someone," Armin pleaded. "That's my greatest desire, after all! I'm not too soft. I can do it! You have no need to doubt me."

Bernd didn't reply. He was confused.

The car pulled into Kassel station, where they had met each other that morning. Armin parked the car and the two men slowly got out and made their way to the station ticket counter.

"A one-way ticket to Berlin on the next available train," Bernd told the woman behind the ticket counter, avoiding Armin's stare.

The woman took little notice of the dark-haired man or his friend as she processed the ticket. Real-life monsters aren't easily identifiable beasts with mad eyes and foaming mouths. Here were two unassuming-looking men. She had no way of guessing their combined appetite for horror.

13

Back from
the Station

Bernd's train back to Berlin was due to leave Kassel in just under twenty minutes. Armin had little time left to earn another chance. The tension between the two men was tangible. Bernd looked down at his shoes and then into the distance, where his train would appear. Armin continually checked the platform clock, as if he could slow time's inevitable progress if he focused enough energy in its direction.

"Do you know where the gents' toilets are?" Bernd asked.

"They're back up in the main station area. You turn right and then there's a sign. Hold on actually, I'll come with you and show you the way."

"No," Bernd said firmly. "I'd prefer it if you waited here, if you don't mind. I need a few minutes by myself."

Bernd headed toward the men's room. He needed a bit of space to collect his thoughts. He had spent almost every moment in Armin's company since he'd first arrived at the station that morning, and he was starting to feel claustrophobic. Worse than that, he was confused. Thoughts sped through his mind. What had he just done? Had he bought a ticket to freedom, an escape from a disastrous situation, from a botched suicide that hadn't even gotten off the ground? Or had he just purchased a train ticket back to the way things always were and had been, namely *hopeless*? Was he now going to return to a humdrum existence and the never-ending frustration of unfulfilled desires? Did Armin lack guts or was it really himself who was the coward?

Bernd reached the bathroom and locked the door. He was glad to be alone. He needed a few moments to reassess the day's events.

He knew one thing: he was tired. His body ached from a lack of nourishment. At least he didn't feel hungry anymore, he consoled himself. The stress of his near suicide bid pressed down on his forehead and he felt the beginnings of another throbbing headache, which threatened to be as bad as the one he'd suffered during his train journey to Kassel. He splashed his face with some cold water and let out a long sigh. That felt better, he thought. He lathered some soap and washed his hands thoroughly. The fog in his brain started to clear. Why was he going home? Could he really face going back to his old life after coming so close to leaving it behind? He looked at himself in the mirror. His face was drawn and he looked pale and tired. Would he ever find another Armin, another man willing to deliver the final stroke to extinguish him? Maybe Armin was his best and last chance. Hadn't Armin seemed to revel in the idea of spilling his blood and eating his guts? Maybe, given the right circumstances, Armin could carry it through after all.

Bernd deliberated for a few minutes and then made up his mind.

Like many a lover, he decided to try again.

Armin anxiously watched Bernd return; there were only ten minutes left before the train to Berlin was due to depart. The platform was rapidly filling up with suitcase-wielding passengers, ready to board the train. "How are you feeling?" he asked cautiously.

"A bit better," Bernd replied. "A lot better in fact." He allowed himself a small smile.

Armin saw his chance.

"Bernd, I honestly think we can do this. I feel such exquisite sexual pleasure when I just *think* about devouring your body parts."

"I need you to be *tough*. Do you think you can castrate me? Please, Armin, I'm begging you. I want it more than anything. This isn't going to work otherwise."

"I'm absolutely convinced I can go through with it." Armin swallowed and said confidently, "Come back to the house with me."

They heard the rumble of train approaching in the distance.

"Okay then," Bernd consented. "Let's give it another go."

The cashier at the station pharmacy paid scarce attention to the men as she scanned through a bottle of cold medicine and a packet of nonprescription sleeping tablets called Vivinox Schlafdragees.

There was no time to waste. Armin kept just within the legal speed limit as he negotiated the city streets. He was in a hurry to get back to the house as soon as possible, and so was Bernd. The cold distance had narrowed between the two, and they were once more resolute in their common goal—the destruction of Bernd's body. Both were ready to wallow in his physical abuse and degradation and, ultimately, in his death.

Bernd rummaged through the shopping bag. They had

made this second round of purchases to be doubly sure they had enough sedatives to knock Bernd out. He shook the bottle of medicine and examined the ingredients and those listed on the side of the sleeping tablets. He read that neither should be taken in combination with alcohol or other medication. Nor should he drive a car or operate heavy machinery while under their influence. Despite having had two doctors as parents, Bernd knew little about drugs or their effects; he just hoped that what they'd bought was strong and would put him to sleep so that Armin could start his butchery.

"Well, there's nothing listed here saying we can't indulge in a bit of cannibalism," he joked. "It just says I can't drive."

"I'm doing the driving," Armin said.

"Well, in that case, I'll risk it." Bernd turned the cap of the 180-milliliter bottle and drank all of its contents in one go. "It doesn't taste too bad," he said. "And now for dessert." He opened the packet of sleeping pills and swallowed ten of the tablets. "Now that's got to work, surely!" he said. "I should be sleeping like a baby cannibal victim in a few hours."

Armin laughed. The atmosphere between them was light again.

The scenery sped past the window as the car made its journey through the state of Hesse. Evening had arrived and commuters were driving home to their country retreats after a hard day's work. Bernd thought of Rene back in Berlin. His partner would no doubt be wondering why he wasn't home from the office by now. But Rene wouldn't get worried for a few hours yet. Then he would probably call Bernd's office to see if he was involved in a lengthy meeting, and would maybe try calling a couple of their friends. Sweet Rene would probably be working out what to cook for dinner. He'd probably want to watch some TV or go out to the movies, Bernd reflected. He sighed; Rene and his life in Berlin seemed a whole world away. He knew their partnership couldn't have survived the complexity of his complete character.

Bernd's insides were crippled with guilt as he thought of Rene having to cope with his loss.

First there would be his disappearance, and then later, when no traces of him were found, the blind acceptance of his death. What he was doing was ultimately selfish, Bernd thought, but then he consoled himself with the thought that Rene would, in time, find himself a better partner, someone worthy of his affections.

Bernd turned his focus back to his impending death. He would feel so liberated when his penis was amputated, it would be the pleasure to end all pleasures. He hoped that he could stay awake long enough to witness its amputation. Would he still be able to hear, at least for a moment, the sound of his own blood gushing from his neck if Armin chopped off his head? He speculated how long a man could stay alive while someone was eating his organs.

Armin was also lost in quiet reflection.

He would have to wash and garnish Bernd's meat well to avoid diseases, he remembered reading on the Internet. He particularly wanted to eat the parts with muscles. Thighs and calves would be his chosen cuts for dinner. He had also read about a tasty stew he could make with the tongue, and a nutritious soup using the eyes. Maybe he could roast chunks of Bernd in the oven too? And what if he ate his heart raw? Hands, feet and testicles really didn't give him much of an appetite. He was glad Bernd wasn't fatty—he would have had to reject him because of potential high cholesterol levels. Bernd was relatively young too, which meant that his flesh shouldn't be too contaminated or tough. How sweet and tender he would taste! But how long would Bernd's delicate meat keep him going for? The food cupboards were relatively empty, and he had some pizzas in the deep freeze, he remembered. If he moved them over, there should be plenty of room to pack in meal-size portions of Bernd . . . His mother had given him rudimentary cooking lessons, and he had picked up recipes over the years of living alone. He wasn't a particularly good chef, but he could cook well enough . . .

The two men drove through the picturesque streets of Rotenburg. The town was a climatic health resort and attracted many tourists. Armin pointed out the town's Renaissance-style castle, the historic marketplace and town hall, and the remains of the old town wall.

When they arrived back at the house, they didn't hesitate before going inside.

They had procrastinated enough.

Armin fetched the bottle of cheap corn Schnapps they had bought on their first trip to the pharmacy at the train station. The alcohol content was over 40 percent, he read on the label. Bernd knocked back half of the bottle, then swallowed another ten sleeping tablets. He was pleased to feel immediately light-headed and slightly nauseous. "I'm a bit drunk!" he said.

They made their way back up to the slaughter room and lay down on the bed. The room spun as Bernd shut his eyes. He felt dizzy as he lifted his head from the pillow to speak. But he was quite clear in his mind as to what he wanted.

"Castrate me, Armin. Then kill me. Now."

14

The
Castration

The alcohol was making Bernd's head spin and it loosened his inhibitions. "Let's listen to some music!" he said giddily. Armin dutifully turned on the portable radio. The two men smoked and listened to music. The atmosphere in the slaughter room was like a bizarre private party. "Come here, you," Armin said flirtatiously to Bernd.

They fell into an embrace. Armin gently stroked Bernd's back and then rubbed his hand up his right thigh. Bernd hadn't eaten in many hours, and he was becoming less capable of rational thought as the chemical cocktail he had taken scrambled his brain. Still, he knew he would attain his ultimate ecstasy from being neutered, not from having sex, and though he felt he would soon pass out, it was essential to him that he at least bear witness to his member being cut off before he grew too groggy from the drugs. He grew impatient with worry. "Do it now, get rid of it," he ordered Armin.

Armin recognized that it would be too difficult to bite off Bernd's penis. He needed an instrument sharper than his teeth—he decided he would use a kitchen knife. Bernd was delighted, as a knife would leave a cleaner cut.

Armin turned his video camera back on. He had carried out numerous amateur amputations on figures made out of marzipan and on plastic dolls. Bernd was only a living human doll, a disposable object whose main worth was his meat. "Cut the thing off," Bernd said once more. This time Armin was ready to oblige. Bernd experienced a state of extreme arousal as he watched Armin pick up the knife and move across the room toward him. *This is it,* he thought, and placed his erect penis on a breadboard, which Armin had brought to the slaughter room for this exact purpose. He adjusted his position so that his full length was exposed.

Armin thought Bernd's sexual organ looked like a stick of salami, ready to be sliced for a tasty sandwich. If he assembled a loaf of bread next to it and squirted the board with some ketchup, he could take an excellent photograph to add to his collection. But he was no longer playing; he gripped the knife handle tighter and raised it above his head. Then he forcefully swung the knife down to the point where Bernd's penis joined his body. ·

Bernd flinched, expecting the blow to sting.

Armin looked down, expecting the penis flesh to be severed.

But nothing had happened; Bernd's penis was still attached to his person. Armin brought the knife down again. He put all his might behind the action. But his efforts were in vain—the knife simply wasn't sharp enough.

Bernd stared down at his penis, uncut and still attached.

"I'm beginning to despair of myself," Armin said.

Bernd refused to be discouraged. The attempts alone were a complete adrenaline high for him. "Go and get a sharper knife," he demanded, sounding imperious and dominant, like Armin's late mother. "Go downstairs to the kitchen and find one!"

As he had always responded to his mother, Armin quickly followed orders and ran down to the kitchen. He returned to the slaughter room, out of breath after running up the stairs, with a chopping knife in his hand. He had checked this blade to ensure it was sharp enough for the amputation. It was six-thirty in the evening.

Armin got into position. This time the unflinching steel came down and hit flesh without mercy.

Bernd let out a terrible scream as the blade hit his body. He yelled as agony surged through to his core. He was jumping around the table and squealing like a pig as Armin brought the knife down again, full force. Bernd shuddered violently and twisted his head from side to side in torment. Armin plunged the knife down again. And again. Bernd rode wave after wave of pain as each deep cut separated more and more of his genitalia from his body. Armin watched Bernd's face as his eyes started to roll back. He reveled in the blood and gore; this was much better than playing with dolls.

At the point when Bernd felt he couldn't take it anymore, he was surprised to suddenly discover it didn't hurt. He felt as if he were somehow removed from his body and floating above the pain as the alcohol and medication kicked in and anesthetized the shock. His body flooded with pleasure as he stared down at his severed organ.

Armin's knife was slippery with blood, but he was able to maintain his grip and use the sharpness to separate some particularly stubborn spots of penis meat from Bernd. Blood streamed down and soaked Bernd's thighs, and he watched with delight as his wound continued to hemorrhage. But he was still awake! He realized that his bleeding had to be slowed if he wanted to accomplish the rest of his dream: eating his own genitalia.

Armin still had bandages from his time in the army. He wrapped some around Bernd to stem the blood loss; it looked like Bernd was wearing a diaper.

"How about an appetizer before your banquet, one that I can share?" Bernd asked. He felt weak as blood continued to flow out of his bandaged wound. But the will to complete his erotic fantasy drove him onward.

"Agreed," Armin replied. He grabbed the blood-soaked meat and the two men rushed downstairs to prepare Bernd's penis for eating.

Once in the kitchen, Armin looked at what he held in his hands. It was as if the glistening, purplish-blue veins still pulsed. He licked the meat until the surface was clean, while Bernd stared transfixated at his severed sex. Then Armin cut the penis into two halves, one for him, and the other for Bernd.

"I hope the meat is succulent," Bernd said.

Armin arranged the meat carefully on his mother's best china plates. "It looks a bit like gourmet cuisine to me," he joked.

Bernd grabbed his portion in his hands and hurriedly tried to gobble it down raw. Armin also picked up his half of the penis and attempted to chew it. But the meat was too tough to bite through. Just like a farm animal's meat, human flesh has to be bled and hung for a few days, Armin reminded his dinner guest. But Bernd had no time to wait; he wanted to devour his own severed penis that instant.

Like the best of hosts, Armin chose to improvise; he fried the hunk of meat, hoping to make it edible for his guest, adding salt, pepper and garlic to taste. He hurried, turning the heat up high. Soon the aroma filled the kitchen. Bernd was so keen to taste his own member that he picked up half and tried—without success—to eat it before it was cooked properly. He had to put it back; then, much to their mutual dismay, the entire penis shriveled in the frying pan and turned black, burning to a cinder.

Armin and Bernd tried in vain to consume it. Ultimately they had to accept that it was lost, that it was too tough for them to digest. Luckily Bernd was still flying high from his amputation. The act had not only satisfied a lust; it was the highest form of sexual satisfaction he had ever experienced. He could take the temporary setback. "I can't wait to be mutilated *again* and eaten," he said.

Armin promised, "If you hold out, we will eat your eggs for breakfast!"

"Eggs" is German slang for testicles.

The promise made Bernd wet his lips.

Bernd felt cold and weak, and the blood leaking from his wound was making a mess. He just wanted to lie in a bath and soak.

Armin continued playing host—he filled his bathtub with warm water and helped Bernd get in. A ring of black filth could be seen around the white bathtub, and it covered the turquoise tiles on the wall; Armin never bothered to clean the bathroom, and dirt had accumulated over the years. Bernd lay back, rested his head on the tub and closed his eyes. It felt so good to have the water warm him. It lessened the terrible chill that was seeping through his bones. The water was soon colored red, and it contrasted sharply with the paleness of his body. Some matter and tissue floated around his motionless body. Bernd had achieved his life's purpose. He could quite happily die now; his life had reached its zenith. Nothing could surpass what he had lived through, and he was still awake enough to taste the sublime pleasure of satisfaction.

His body did its best to heal itself. Every now and again, the wound would seal up enough to stop the flow of blood. But Bernd amused himself by fiddling with the large, bloody hole where his penis used to be, to ensure that the fatal fountain continued. The red flood of liquid that streamed out of his wound hypnotized him. *I look like one of those stone statues in fountains*, he thought to himself, *spurting blood instead of water*.

Armin left Bernd alone. He still could save Bernd's life if he called for an ambulance. But he wasn't interested in saving Bernd. His plan was working out perfectly.

Bernd lay in the bath and felt the world slip away. He wondered what it would feel like to be eaten alive. *Would the pleasure match that which he'd experienced earlier?* Reality retreated and fantasy advanced as he started to lose his grip on life. He imagined that he was lying in a giant cooking pot, being boiled alive. He pictured hordes of teeth bearing down on him to tear apart his flesh. They chewed slowly, with a sawing motion, the way a shark feeds, and then ripped and shredded the rest of his body into tiny pieces. He started muttering aloud, and Armin, hearing his voice, came back to the bathroom.

He was surprised to see the extreme pallor of Bernd's face; there was a blue tinge starting to spread across his chalk-white skin, and his lips were violet. He looked nothing like the healthy specimen who had turned up at the train station that morning. But Bernd wore a happy expression, and he seemed at peace. Armin wondered how much longer he would have to wait before he could seek his own ultimate pleasure.

"You've no idea how good this feels," Bernd muttered, realizing Armin was near. "You've no idea how glad I am about this. It's the most pleasure I've ever had. It's what I always wanted."

Armin didn't truly comprehend his victim's feeling of

elation caused by the amputation of his sex organ. Nor did he really want to. He had fulfilled his part of the bargain. Now he could slaughter and eat Bernd so that he could have a real companion, someone to stay with him always. "I'm sure I'll feel just as good when I eat you," he said. "Then you can rise again in me and be with me always."

But Bernd didn't want to rise again. "I don't want anything to remain of me," he said. "I want you to ground up my skull and my teeth so there is absolutely *nothing* left." He wanted to make himself clear. "I want to be *completely annihilated*," he said with as much strength as he could muster.

Armin reassured his meal. "Don't worry, I'll look after the waste," he said.

Bernd smiled, and sank back further in the bath. It was so cold. He buried his shoulders under the warm water, wrapping it around him like a cloak. His pulse was slowing. Death was creeping near.

The view of Armin's house from the lane. Locals called it "the haunted house" because it was so dilapidated; his mother called it her "country estate."

Photo © Lois Jones

The yard was full of broken-down cars that Armin never got around to fixing.

Photo © Lois Jones

The garden was full of trash; Armin did not maintain the estate.

Photo © Lois Jones

The inside of Armin's house was a shambles; he spent most of his time in front of his computers, surfing cannibal sites on the Internet.

Photo © Rabsch

Armin's mother was a stern disciplinarian. After she died, his cannibalistic fantasies became more concrete and more brutal.

Photo © Lantelme

Bernd Juergen Brandes wrote to Armin in an email "There's absolutely no way back for me, only forwards through your teeth." It was his dream to be castrated, and to be eaten alive.

Photo © Lantelme

An exterior shot of Kassel-Wilhelmshöhe train station, where Armin collected his victim, Bernd Juergen Brandes. *Photo © Lois Jones*

Armin's self-built slaughter room. The electric heaters were placed in the room when one potential victim requested he be "barbecued alive"; the cage was used to accommodate another potential victim's fantasies. *Photo © Rabsch*

The bed in the slaughter room where Armin could chain down those who answered his "slaughter boy" ads, and the whip he made. *Photo © Rabsch*

The filthy bath in which Bernd lay, bleeding, after the amputation of his penis.
Photo © Rabsch

A hook in the ceiling of the human abattoir; Armin suspended several potential victims who changed their minds and were set free. Ultimately, he hung Bernd's body from a hook in his home-built slaughter room.
Photo © Rabsch

Interior of the freezer unit used to store Bernd Juergen Brandes. A frozen pizza and a dead rat were the only other contents found by the police.
Photo © Rabsch

Police made their way to Armin's home after receiving a tip given to them by a web-surfing college student.

Photo © Lantelme

The saw used to cut up Bernd Juergen Brandes's body.

Photo © Lantelme

Investigators searched the grounds of Armin's estate thoroughly, looking for Bernd's remains—and the remains of any other victims.

Photo © Lantelme

Günther Küllmer, the lead detective investigating the case of the "real-life Hannibal Lecter." *Photo © Lantelme*

Armin attended court each day looking calm and well-dressed. He spoke to the court with his hands crossed in front of him. Spectators were disappointed that he was so normal looking. *Photo © Lantelme*

The court case of "The Cannibal of Rotenburg" caused a worldwide sensation. *Photo © Lantelme*

The quiet life of Armin's neighbors was shattered during the trial, and after the shocking verdict.

Photo © Lantelme

Armin "The Cannibal" has adjusted well to life behind bars; here he is, pictured in prison.

Photo © Rabsch

15

Bernd
Continues
to Live

Bernd lay in the bath, as motionless as a corpse. His eyes were closed and the hint of a smile played on his lips. A river of blood washed around him, the water turning a deeper shade of red as blood continued to flow out of the severed stump that used to be his penis. Armin stared at him.

It had been over an hour since he had last come into the bathroom, and his guest's condition had clearly deteriorated during that time. Bernd now looked like a life-size mannequin; he was a body just waiting to be lacerated and pulled apart, then chopped up into edible pieces. Armin longed to start his work, the rendering of Bernd into chunks of meat to consume. He could still taste Bernd's flesh on his tongue. It was a shame it had been too tough to chew. He was greedy for more.

This time, he would properly prepare the meat.

Good cooking shouldn't be rushed.

Was Bernd dead already? Armin moved quietly to the

side of the bath and closely watched for signs of life, for a slight movement or the flicker of an eyelid. But Bernd lay stock-still in the water, marinating in his body's own juices. Armin stretched out his finger and gingerly touched Bernd's chest. There was no reaction. His skin felt cold, too. Armin tried again, this time poking Bernd harder. He jumped back, startled, as Bernd stirred and let out a long groan. Bernd wasn't dead yet, after all.

"Bernd, are you all right?" Armin inquired. "Can you hear me?"

Bernd attempted to lift his head from the back of the bath. The world started to spin; he laid his head down on the cool, steady surface. He waited until the dizziness eased, then tried again. He inched his head upward, feeling as if his brains had been replaced with lead weights that were chained to the bath, pulling him back down. For a moment, he wondered if he were really in the gym, lying on the press-up bench. All the weights must have fallen on top of him and he couldn't lift them to get up, he thought. How did that happen? Maybe one of the instructors would come past and free him. His head filled up with delusional notions, until Armin's voice woke him from his trance. "Bernd? Speak to me. Say something."

Bernd tried to remember who owned the voice that was talking to him. He knew it, for sure. *But who was it?* Curiosity pulled open his eyes. He focused on the bathroom tiles until they weren't blurred anymore, and then looked at the man next to him. He looked familiar. *Ah, Armin, of course!* That was right, he was in Armin's old farmhouse. *But what was he doing in the bath and why was the water red?* The day's events flooded back. He recollected his recent castration and murmured a sigh of delight as he gazed down at his wound. He had been sterilized, gelded like an animal! He wasn't a man anymore. His manhood had been removed for good. He dug into the wound and jumped as the shock made him lucid again.

"Armin," he said weakly. "Hello, yes, I'm still here."

"How do you feel?" Armin asked. "Are you in a lot of pain?"

"No, I just feel tired and weak," Bernd replied. "I don't seem to have any energy left. Have I been here long?"

"A good couple of hours," Armin replied. "The bathwater is stone cold. Do you want me to add some warm water? Or is there anything I can bring you?"

"I'd like a glass of drinking water," Bernd said, moving his tongue through his dehydrated mouth. "I'm really thirsty. And I think I really want to go to sleep for a little while. I'm so dreadfully tired. That's all I want really."

"Shall I move you to the bed then? Maybe you'll be more comfortable there?" *And you'll also be nearer the slaughter table.* Armin understood that it would be easier to move Bernd now, while he was still alive, rather than shifting a dead body later.

Bernd smiled. "Yes please. I'd like that." His body longed to collapse into a soft mattress, and hide under the warmth of thick covers. He imagined his head sinking into a big pillow, full of feathers. It would be so comfortable. He would just melt into the bed. He was likely too weak by now to remember or care about the sordid state of the old bed and the smell of rotten vegetables that emanated from its damp blankets. Armin helped Bernd slowly lift his upper body into an upright position, then put his arms around his bloodstained torso and heaved him out of the bath. He staggered backward as Bernd collapsed his full weight against him. "Come on, Bernd, you've got to help me," Armin urged gently. "Let's do this together."

"I'll do my best." Bernd felt as if his voice were coming from a long way away.

Bernd extended his legs and took a few steps forward. He faltered, uncertain of his feet, then steadied himself and straightened up. Silver dots speckled in front of his eyes. "That's it, you're doing great," Armin said. "Take some more steps forward and lean against me. We haven't got far to go."

Bernd moved one foot forward and supported his weight against Armin. He felt as if he were running a marathon. His body wanted to pack in; he'd had enough. It was only his self-determination that kept him going.

The men crossed the landing and headed toward the abattoir. Bernd could see the door open in front of him. He concentrated on placing one foot in front of the other to reach his goal.

"It's not far now," Armin encouraged. "You know you can do it."

"Let me stop a second and catch my breath," Bernd begged.

They stopped for a few minutes before setting off again, at an agonizingly slow pace. When at last they reached the cell-like room, Bernd collapsed into a heap on the bed. Armin covered him with the bedclothes and plumped up the sordid pillows beneath his head, as if he were tucking in a child after a bedtime story. Bernd closed his eyes, grateful not to have to move anymore. He let his mind escape and flee his dying body.

Armin tiptoed out of the room. He would check on Bernd every half hour. In the meantime, he would watch television. He aimlessly flicked through the TV channels, but nothing looked interesting. He channel hopped for a while and tried to lose his thoughts in the bright images that danced across the screen. Soon, the television faded into background noise as he began to plan out in his mind all the details of the upcoming slaughter.

• • •

Armin checked his watch. Thirty minutes had passed since he had put Bernd to bed. He needed to check on him, to see if he was still alive.

Bernd's condition remained stable. He was weak, but he was still breathing. Armin could see his chest moving up and down.

Armin retreated downstairs. He couldn't be bothered trying to watch the TV again. He needed something that would really take his mind off things and make the time pass more quickly. He decided to read one of his *Star Trek* novels. He had always found it easy to lose himself in the world of fantasy portrayed in the series.

Another half hour went by. Armin checked Bernd's pulse. He could feel a regular beat. He measured Bernd's pulse against his own. Bernd's was slower, but maintained a constant rhythm. Bernd moved his lips in response to touch, but Armin couldn't catch his words.

Armin left the room and kicked the door shut in frustration.

Bernd's dying was taking such an awfully long time! He didn't know how much longer he could wait. How slowly time seemed to be passing! He willed the fingers on his watch to inch forward. The past hour had seemed to take an eternity. He wished Bernd would hurry up and die! He returned to the living room, slumped back on the sofa and moodily picked up his book again. He tried to surrender himself to the world of *Star Trek*. He'd read this story before, and it was one of his favorites.

Armin chuckled as he poured over details of the crew's adventures on other planets. He wondered if there were planets out there where cannibalism was allowed. He decided that if he had a spaceship, he would find a planet where all the best restaurants served human flesh and all the noble families sat down and dined upon other human beings each night. They would have the unchallenged power to do so and everyone would relish the taste. Only the poor people would have to eat prey with four legs. There would be special butchers' shops and a range of delicious cannibal recipes. And on this planet, he wouldn't have to hide his desires. He would be accepted and popular. Even his mother would approve of his man-eating habits, and would admire him because of it. He pictured acres of young flesh where consumers would be given a razor blade to shave off slices off young boys' buttocks to sample their flesh before deciding which one they would like to have cooked for dinner.

Soon some of that could happen on this planet. He glanced down at his watch. Another forty minutes had passed. It was past time to check on Bernd.

Armin slowly opened the door to Bernd's temporary bedroom. He was surprised to see that Bernd was now awake; he had shifted his position on to his side and watched Armin enter the room.

"I'm glad you're here," Bernd said in a faint voice. "I'm desperate to use the toilet. I was dreaming about it and then I woke up. I really need to urinate but I don't know if I can anymore. Do you think it's possible?"

Armin thought for a moment. "I don't see why not. I mean, you've still got the tubes there even if your penis isn't. It should still work."

"Would you help me then?" Bernd replied. "I haven't got any strength left to do it by myself."

Armin lifted Bernd out of the bed and supported his weight. Bernd staggered to the bathroom, leaning on Armin. He relieved his bladder with Armin's assistance. It should have hurt, but by now Bernd seemed too drugged to notice pain.

"It's strange how the body keeps on functioning even

after an operation like yours, isn't it?" Armin remarked. "It's remarkable really."

Bernd nodded his agreement. Talking cost him too much effort. He just wanted to fall back into bed and fall out of life. He knew that he had reached the twilight hours of his days. Soon the light would be turned off forever. He was happy not to fight it. He wondered if heaven really existed, if there were an afterlife, where he could be reunited with his mother. No, he decided. His story was reaching its end. Once he had left this life, then nothing would remain. Bernd Juergen Brandes would be no more. Annihilated. Extinguished. "I don't think I'm going be here much longer," he said quietly. "I can feel myself slipping away."

"I know," Armin replied.

"I'm weak, very weak. I feel like I'm about to run out of power. But I'm happy. It's what I want. I'll be gone soon."

Armin smiled. "Is there anything else you want or need?"

"Any last requests, you mean?" Bernd said.

"Yes, I guess so."

Bernd closed his eyes for a moment. Darkness was filling up behind his eyelids. He thought he could hear distant voices speaking to him in silvery tongues. It was a melodic sound, a language that he had never heard before, but somehow it seemed familiar. Then again, maybe it was just the sound of the wind in the trees outside the window.

"Yes, I know what you can do for me. I want you to wait until I've lost consciousness. Then I want you to slash my throat. But only after I'm unconscious, not beforehand. I've lost so much blood, I don't think it will be much longer before I pass out."

Armin was more than happy to agree. He longed to plunge a cold, metallic blade deep into Bernd's throat and see the blood gush out. He looked down at the blood-slick wound and the torn flesh where he had castrated Bernd. He wondered how much blood Bernd had lost, and how much a man could bleed before he died, or at least lost consciousness. Bernd was deathly pale now.

"It's time soon, it's time," Armin said.

"Yes," Bernd replied. "At last. You won't have to wait much longer now, my friend, for your flesh."

16

The
Difficult
Part

Bernd finally slipped into unconsciousness at 3:30 A.M.

Armin came in for his routine check, and gazed down at an inert body. Bernd looked heavier somehow, and colder. Armin tried pinching him to see if he was truly unconscious. There was no response. He lifted one of Bernd's eyelids and snapped his fingers close to his ear. Still nothing.

Armin was delighted.

"You're out cold, aren't you, Bernd?" he said loudly.

When Bernd failed to answer or wake up, Armin rushed out of the room, infused with fresh energy and vigor. He needed to change into his chosen slaughter outfit: a pair of dark blue pajamas, Wellington boots and a bedsheet belonging to his dead mother, which he wrapped around himself and wore as an apron.

He didn't want any blood to splatter on his best pajamas.

Armin was ready to start work. He snapped his fingers a

few times as he tried to remember all the things he had to do. *The video, of course,* he thought. *I've got to start the video again to film the slaughter.* He went to the slaughter room and turned on the video camera. He didn't plan to make money with the filmed butchery; he was creating the video only for himself. He hoped the images would allow him to relive what was soon to be the most triumphant moment of his life. This slaughter would be an exercise in ultimate control, and Armin planned on prolonging the delicious feelings by re-viewing the video. He couldn't believe the moment had finally arrived. His excitement grew as he hauled Bernd's naked body from the bed onto the slaughter bench. Bernd was heavy and it was awkward, but the thrill of the imminent act of butchery gave Armin extra strength. He pushed Bernd to the center of the table and arranged his limbs so he was lying with his arms and legs stretched out and his face directed upward. There was his willing slaughter boy. What a fine specimen of a man, Armin told himself, as he looked down at the body. He had chosen well.

Bernd's chest gently moved up and down; he was still breathing.

Armin checked his pulse. It was racing.

Bernd's lips were moving slightly, as if he were reciting a silent prayer. Armin felt a knot tighten in his stomach. He was scared of this part, the killing part; he would have preferred it if Bernd had jumped out of the window or had hung himself. Then he'd just have to chop up the body before eating it. However, the meat could have been bruised and damaged if Bernd had injured himself, and Armin knew he didn't want spoiled goods; he wanted prime, succulent meat. And he *would* have it; he just had to kill to make it happen. "I have to do it," he told himself. "I have to go through with it."

Bernd *looked* dead, stock still, covered in blood, with

bluish tones to his skin, but his chest was visibly moving up and down, indicating he was still alive.

Armin checked that Bernd's eyes were completely shut and kissed him. He took a few deep breaths. *There's no going back now.* He planted another lingering kiss on Bernd's mouth. He caught a taste of Bernd, reminding him of the hot kisses they had exchanged the day before, when their limbs wrapped around each other in passion. He instantly pushed the memory out of his mind. He couldn't afford to grow sentimental. The killing was a necessary evil; it was a means to an end. Armin let out a deep breath. "Goodbye, my dear friend. It's time to say farewell."

Armin was struck by the sanctity of the moment; he recalled his mother's death and her funeral, with his brothers and his father. He tried to recollect some of the priest's words during the service. The priest had said something about his mother leading a good life, and then he had blessed her in the next one. Armin decided to say a prayer to pay his last respects to Bernd and give him a proper funeral celebration. He folded his hands in a prayer position. "Almighty Father, thank you for creating this man who lies before me. Thank you for allowing me to prolong his life by letting his spirit live on inside me by consuming his body after his death. May my friend have a nice death, and may all his relatives and his loved ones continue to lead happy lives and be blessed on this earth.

"Bernd Juergen Brandes was, as far as I knew him, a good man, and was intelligent and kind. May he be remembered as such. He chose to give me a great gift, and for that, I will be eternally grateful." Armin paused as he searched for the right words. The next bit was the difficult part. "Please, God, forgive me for the act I'm about to carry out. I don't know how it looks in your all-seeing eyes, but I hope you understand why I'm doing it. I plead for forgiveness for all my sins, and particularly for the sin I'm about to commit. Amen."

Armin's hands trembled badly as he picked up a long-handled kitchen knife. He gripped the handle so hard it left an imprint on his skin. It was a large knife; the blade measured eighteen centimeters long. Armin held Bernd's head and stabbed his pale throat. He heard the blood flow and then drip on the floor. With several stabs to the throat, he killed Bernd.

The whole thing lasted about three minutes.

It had taken nine-and-a half hours for Bernd to die, since his penis had been cut off. Armin laughed in disbelief. He no longer felt like a harmless inadequate; now he felt like the most powerful man in the world. He was superior to all others, he was the best! He was a man who had just *stabbed someone to death!* He yelled out: "Yes!" His voice sounded loud and strong. He couldn't believe he had gone ahead and done it! He had actually killed a man! He turned toward the corpse; he wanted Bernd to share in his happiness. "This is an *incredible* feeling for me. My life's dream has come true."

Armin was then deluged by a series of conflicting emotions.

The first was hatred; he repulsed himself for going ahead with the slaying. He despised Bernd for consenting to it. Then he felt anger. He was furious that his fondness for human flesh and his inability to ignore his perverse fantasies had driven him to such extremes. The third emotion he felt was guilt. His subconscious told him he had committed a crime that would be considered murder in some people's eyes. A voice inside reminded him that life was something sacred; a gift to treasure, not destroy. *But Bernd had been a willing participant in his own death. . . .*

Armin talked to himself to vindicate his actions. "I didn't want to kill or hurt anybody. Bernd came to me of his own free will to end his life. For him, it was a nice death. I only did what he wanted, what he asked me to do."

Feelings of regret soon added to Armin's guilt. His biggest regret was that he hadn't got to know Bernd better before stabbing him to death, since he seemed such a nice man.

But the negative emotions were soon supplanted.

Strong feelings of joy and arousal coursed through Armin and he became ecstatic as he savored the power he held over the dead body. Once again he felt strong and invincible. He had a body that was his to do with as he pleased! He had *really* completed his life's dream! Not many people could claim that, he thought proudly. "I had the fantasy and in the end I fulfilled it," he said, with a smile.

He had found his blood brother and had killed him.

Now all he had to do was chop him up and devour him, piece by piece.

Armin believed Bernd's flesh would survive inside him after he had assimilated it, just as other's flesh survived when the eye or the heart of a dead man was donated to a living man. It would be like an organ donation, but with spiritual overtones. The consumption of Bernd's flesh would be more than just a physical act; it would be the merging of two souls. Armin felt as though he had just gotten married to Bernd, not killed him.

"I feel fulfilled—like I'm married to you," he whispered to Bernd's carcass, affectionately stroking his dead face. "I won't care if I go to prison or am punished for this, as long as I can remember this moment."

Armin was feeling extreme sexual arousal; though not because of the sex he and Bernd had shared. What was turning Armin on was the prospect of eating the cadaver that lay on the butcher's table before him. Consuming Bernd's body would be a heightened form of intimacy, more elevated than the sexual act. He wanted to sort out the inside parts of Bernd's body and place them neatly in order. He felt the sweetest, erotic thrill at the prospect of swallowing Bernd's meat. He took enormous pleasure in the thought of cooking and then digesting his first human steak. "I bet you can't wait for me to eat you, can you!" he said to Bernd in a playful tone.

"Oh, you lucky thing. You lucky, lucky man. This is the best thing ever."

17

The
Gein
Configuration

Armin softly stroked the side of Bernd's dead face. The skin felt cold beneath his fingers. He was overcome by a wave of tenderness toward Bernd; this was his soul mate and he wanted to memorize his features. Especially since Bernd's face would no longer be recognizable once it had been skinned.

"Bernd, it's time for your loving, cannibalistic funeral celebration, my friend," he said. "Your body won't have to waste away in the ground or be burned to a cinder. I know you didn't want that."

Armin pulled Bernd's body slightly toward him on the butcher's bench. He felt big and strong as he stood over the body. This was an awesome demonstration of power for him. Soon he would satisfy his sexual desire to eat a man, or long pig, as it had been referred to throughout its culinary history. Armin hoped the flesh on the well-exercised body would be tender. A certain amount of fat was desirable as marbling to add a juicy, flavorful quality, and it looked like Bernd had just about enough fat on him.

Armin rubbed his hand along the corpse's thighs as he talked to his dead friend. "I can't wait to sink my teeth into these taut thighs and your plump, ready-to-eat rump. Soon I'll be able to butcher and eat your horny flesh." He looked at his watch. It wouldn't be an easy job to break down the human body from the full figure into serviceable choice cuts of meat. He had better get started. It was time for Bernd to be hoisted.

Armin suspended the corpse upside down from a meat hook to gut it and clean it.

He hauled the feet up first, with the head down so that the body could bleed dry, like a pig. This was called the Gein configuration, and he had learned it from the cannibal sites online. He tied simple loops of rope around the hands and placed the arms out of the way so that he could access the torso easily. *And now let's start the bleeding.* Armin placed a large open vessel beneath Bernd's head, gripped his long kitchen knife and plunged it in about an inch at one corner of the jaw. It was amazing to feel the blade sink into the flesh. He looked proudly at his first incision. Then he made a deep ear-to-ear cut through the neck and larynx to the opposite side, elongating the earlier, fatal cut to Bernd's throat. He knew this would sever the internal and external major arteries, which carried blood from the heart to the head, face and brain. He stepped back from the cadaver as Bernd's blood poured out. After the initial rush, the stream died down and Armin directed the blood into a container. He watched as the red fluid poured out. Then he massaged the corpse's extremities down toward the trunk and pumped the stomach to drain out the rest of the blood. He knew from his reading that a mature long pig like Bernd should normally contain about six liters of blood.

Still, he couldn't believe how much blood seemed to flow out of him—even after his castration.

The red river flowing out of Bernd finally started to ease. Armin stared at the bucket full of blood and the blood-splattered floor and walls. He would have to dispose of the bucket somewhere.

Now that the bleeding was done, Armin geared himself up to chop off his dead friend's head. He sliced away the neck muscle and ligament, then he cleanly removed the head by gripping it on either side and twisting it off where the spinal cord met the skull.

Armin contemplated Bernd's severed head. He had heard human brain wasn't that good to eat; he also knew that the large brain mass was hard to remove without opening the skull. Cannibal folklore had taught him to place the skull outside in a wire cage so that scavengers such as ants and maggots could cleanse the flesh from the bones. A more realistic option, given his circumstances, was to saw the skull to get at the brains, although that would demand a lot of physical strength. No, he decided, he wouldn't do that. He would keep the skull intact. Bernd should join in the fun. He had enjoyed chatting to him, and realized he didn't want to stop now.

Armin grabbed Bernd's head by the hair and placed it on the table so that he could talk to it as he disemboweled its body.

"There you are, Bernd," he said to the severed head. "Now you can watch. You wanted to watch, didn't you?" The eyes were closed, but Armin spoke with the severed head as if it could see. He continued his bloody work, saying, "You don't need to be worried. You're going to be just fine."

The next stage in the slaughter was the skinning of Bernd's hide. Armin wanted to flay the carcass so that he could expose Bernd's muscular configuration and get rid of the hair and the tiny glands that produced sweat and oil; they looked distasteful. He knew skin was composed of two layers: an outer thinner one, with a thicker tissue layer below it. He first scored the skin's surface, cutting lightly to be sure of depth and direction, and then cut down into the skin tissue.

He cut long slices about an inch apart and started peeling away each layer of skin. It was slow work. On the fattier parts, he carefully pulled the skin from the fat underneath. He shivered with pleasure as it made a pronounced ripping noise. Armin gazed longingly at the exposed red flesh. Next, he tore Bernd's scrotum away from his body.

He addressed the severed head, "I bet you're sorry you won't be able to join me eating these for breakfast, aren't you, Bernd?"

Now that he'd removed the skin, Armin could start gutting the carcass. He made a cut from the solar plexus, between the breastbone and stomach, almost to the anus. He was careful not to cut into the intestines; he didn't want to contaminate the surrounding area with feces or bacteria. He then ran his blade around the anus and tied it off with twine. This also prevented contamination, as it stopped the body from voiding any material left in the bowel.

Armin used his saw to cut through the pubic bones. The lower body now lay completely open, and he began to pull out the organ masses. He let out a long sigh of pleasure as he grabbed huge handfuls of the large and small intestines, kidneys, liver and stomach and cut them away from the back wall of the body. He loved the feel of the slippery masses of flesh in his hands. He marveled how these had once served as part of the engine driving Bernd's body.

Armin was in heaven as he disemboweled his friend. He felt such tremendous power; Bernd's body was his to do with as he wished. Everything was going according to plan. After spending hours pouring over cannibal Web sites, he knew by heart the best methods to eviscerate a carcass—all he had to do was put his knowledge into practice.

Armin heard a quiet click and jumped. He stalled a moment, confused as to where the sound was coming from. He looked at Bernd's skull, as if he expected the decapitated head to offer an explanation. *Ah, the video camera*, he suddenly realized. He bounded across the room to check his equipment.

The videotape had run out.

He felt a surge of annoyance; it was essential to film the slaughter so he could freeze his moment of glory. Blood and guts spilled onto the floor as Armin stepped out of his slaughter outfit. Bits of Bernd seemed to be everywhere. Armin stepped around the mess and went to the sink to wash his hands. He scrubbed them clean of blood, splashed water on his face and put on a change of clothing. "There, that's better," he said.

He left the mutilated body and calmly drove to Rotenburg to buy another videotape.

Armin strolled in a relaxed way through the streets of Rotenburg. He barely noticed paying for the videotape or getting back into his car; his thoughts were focused on his abattoir. He couldn't wait to start chopping up Bernd's upper torso. When he arrived back at the farm, he ran up the stairs, inserted the new cassette in the recorder and put his blood-soaked clothes back on.

He turned to the skull. "I'm home, Bernd. Hope you weren't too lonely while I was gone."

Armin resumed his work, now cutting through the diaphragm of the carcass. The muscular membrane divided the upper and the lower abdominal cavities. He removed the breastbone, cutting down to the point on each side where it connected to the ribs, and then sawing through and detaching it from the collarbone. He pulled out Bernd's heart and held it high above his head, in a gesture of triumph. He took out the lungs and removed the larynx and trachea from Bernd's cut throat.

"So now I've taken out all the inner organs," he said in a satisfied tone.

He trimmed away the blood vessels and any remaining pieces of connective tissue from the interior of the carcass and washed it out.

He was now ready to start the actual butchering of the body.

Armin cut into the armpit and bored straight through to the shoulder. He removed the arm bone from the collarbone and shoulder blade, before chopping the hand off an inch or so above the wrist. Most of the meat would be between the elbow and the shoulder, where the muscle groups were larger. He broke apart the elbow joint; the two halves of the arm looked perfect to carve servings from.

His next task was to split the body. He removed the entire backbone by cutting and then sawing up either side from the tailbone. He then took down the two halves and chopped off the feet about three inches up from the ankle. The bones thickened where the leg connected to the foot.

It was tough work.

Armin then divided each side of meat into two more main portions: the ribs and the shoulder; and the half-pelvis and leg. In between was the belly, which he planned to use for fillets and steaks, or thin strips for bacon. He decided to roll some of the wide strips of flesh to serve as a roast. The ribs would be delicious when barbecued.

He moved on to one of the top quarters of the carcass. He trimmed away the neck and cut along the outline of the shoulder blade, removing the meat on top and dislocating the large bone. He made an incision along the length of the collarbone and then cut and pried it away.

"Oh, that's a lovely piece of meat, Bernd," he said.

Then he cut the lower quarters. This was where most of the meat was. The muscle mass was largest in the legs and rump. The main pieces were the buttock, or rump, and the upper leg, or thigh. He removed the whole calf muscle from the back of the lower legs and admired the cut. All those hours Bernd had spent cycling and in the gym had paid off. Armin cut off the leg at the bottom of the rump, then chopped away the bony knee mass. He spoke again to the head. "Your upper leg is ready to be made into beautifully thick, round steaks, my dear." He carved Bernd's buttocks from the pelvis. The thighs provided the rest of the meat.

And that was basically it.

Armin stood back and proudly examined his work. The whole process had taken a few hours, but he had cut off a lot of flesh.

A veritable feast lay before him.

All he had to do now was dispose of the offal and other waste trimmings. He grabbed a handful of gut and slipped it into the waste bucket, making a wet plop.

"You'll soon become one with me, dear friend," he said.

18

The
Biggest
Kick
in My Life

Armin stood in the garden, absorbed in quiet reflection. His thoughts transported him back to his mother's funeral. He felt a twinge of pain as he recollected her coffin being gently lowered into the ground, and the emptiness he had felt after her death. This time, though, he wouldn't be abandoned. This time his friend could rejoin him forever in body and spirit.

Armin grabbed a spade and started digging a deep hole in his neglected garden, loosening stones and weeds from the ground as he turned over the soil. He needed to dig a grave before the funeral service could commence. His chosen burial ground for Bernd's bones, skin and innards lay next to the spot where he had buried his Alsation. The rest of Bernd's savaged body lay in pieces in the kitchen, destined for the cooking pot, not the burial ground. And Bernd's skull wasn't included in the parts being buried—Armin couldn't quite bring himself to part with it. He would bury the skull at a later date, he promised himself. In the meantime, Bernd's cranium could live in the freezer.

Once the makeshift grave was ready, Armin solemnly placed his hands in a prayer position and bowed his head forward. He chose to recite the words of Psalm 23 for the impromptu service; it was one of his favorites and the words always soothed him. He recited from memory, in a clear voice: "The Lord is my shepherd; I shall not want. He maketh me to lie down in green pastures: he leadeth me beside the still waters." He solemnly threw Bernd's body parts into the grave as he continued to deliver the psalm in as dignified a manner as he could muster. "Surely goodness and mercy shall follow me all the days of my life: and I will dwell in the house of the Lord for ever," he concluded, as he tossed in the last of Bernd's remains. Then he quietly said the words to the Lord's Prayer. "Our Father who art in heaven, hallowed be thy name. Thy kingdom come. Thy will be done, as in heaven, so in earth. Give us day by day our daily bread." Even though he had recited the prayer daily in grammar school, he paused and stuttered as he reached the second part of the prayer. "And forgive us our sins; for we also forgive every one that is indebted to us. And lead us not into temptation, but deliver us from evil."

Would he be forgiven his sins? Or would he be eternally damned? He knew he wasn't the first to sample human flesh; his primeval ancestors had regularly eaten their friends and foes. But would he be punished for reawakening a primeval presence from the dark past of the human mind? Or would he be allowed to live in peace for the rest of his life, content at having lived out his dream? Armin dismissed thoughts of sin and redemption from his mind— it was too big a topic for him to grasp at the moment.

He picked up the shovel and slowly started throwing soil onto the grave, until he had covered the scant physical leftovers of Bernd's body. He threw in a symbolic last handful of soil, spreading his fingers wide as he watched the grains trickle through them onto the grave. He used the spade to flatten and smooth the grave's surface. It really needed a flower or a cross, but he didn't want to risk drawing attention to it. Hopefully, it would remain unnoticed by neighbors and visitors to the house. Flowers—and grass— would eventually grow over it.

The funeral had reached its end.

The service would be followed by a buffet of the deceased.

"Farewell, my friend," Armin said, and turned and walked back into the house.

Armin set about hacksawing the human flesh he had harvested into meal-size portions.

He loved the touch of the slippery meat in his hands. He grasped handfuls of it and raised it to his lips and nose. His appetite grew as he imagined a whole piece of flesh entering his body. He delighted in identifying the parts that lay before him, and remembering what they had looked like on Bernd while he was still alive. He meticulously sorted out the various cuts on his kitchen table, before neatly labeling them "rump," "steak," "fillet," "ham" and "bacon."

"Oh, I've got some delicious meals ahead of me, I can see already," he said excitedly.

He packed the servings of meat into plastic storage bags and arranged them in the freezer, next to a frozen pizza. He was delighted to see that he had enough meals to keep him going for quite a while. And such a variety of cuts! It would save on his grocery bill—all he needed to buy was some vegetables and pasta as side dishes and he would have enough food to eat for the next few months!

Armin's excitement grew as he anticipated his first meal

of human flesh. He knew that he needed to be patient and wait a couple of days for the meat to cure before eating it. In the meantime, he staved off hunger pangs by snacking on chips and pretzels and eating tinned tomato soup.

He pondered which piece of meat to cut and cook first. Maybe he would put a roast in the oven, or fry a big, juicy steak? When the weather started to get better, he could make hamburgers and rissoles from Bernd and barbecue them on the grill. He could also take meatballs into work to eat for lunch. He could cut up thin strips of human flesh and use them in a stir-fry, or make mincemeat for a spaghetti Bolognese . . . the possibilities for meals were endless.

Armin decided to save one of Bernd's arms and one of his feet. He wanted to experiment a little. He cooked the arm in the oven to dry it out, planning to hang it up in the kitchen like the air-dried hams of Parma in Italy. Unfortunately, the aesthetic impact of Bernd's shriveled limb wasn't the same as the Italian hams, so he decided to grind it up instead to make flour. He kept the bone meal that the arm produced in an old bread bin. He was sure that he would find a use for it one day. He was determined to be more creative with Bernd's severed foot.

He boiled it whole in a pot, then placed the cooked foot on a plate, rubbed ketchup over it to give the illusion of blood and decorated it with herbs. He filled a bowl with boiling water and placed it behind the adorned foot; he wanted to make it look as if steam was rising from the severed appendage. He gazed at the boiled foot. He was proud of his artistic effort, but he had no desire to eat it. The foot didn't give him an appetite; he derived pleasure just from looking at the bizarre composition. This real human part was so much better than his life-size marzipan creations had been. He took photos, convinced they would give foot fetishists a thrill. He wondered if people would realize that they were looking at a real dead man's foot, once he published the pictures online. Personally, he found it difficult to understand people's erotic obsession with feet—he didn't find them at all arousing. Unlike freshly slaughtered flesh . . .

Armin prepared for the meal ahead. He couldn't remember when he had last felt so happy, so high and so powerful. Nothing in life seemed out of his reach anymore. He was sure that he would carry the memories of the previous day's events with him always. To his grave, in fact.

And he still had the video to watch to relive his triumph! Three videocassettes, to be exact, lasting over four hours. He put on the first, and watched as he and Bernd moved across the screen. It was strange to watch himself, and stranger to listen to himself talk. He was surprised to hear how his voice sounded. The video refreshed each moment of the day's events in his memory, and as he watched himself live out his most cherished fantasies, he felt sexually aroused for the first time since the slaughter. He felt the beginnings of an erection, which he improved with his hand. He had to masturbate when he saw the slaughter scenes, he found the brutal carnage so erotic. He was soon covered in sweat and moaning with pleasure as he watched himself pull out Bernd's innards on the video. He hit the pause button time and again to relive his favorite scenes; he stimulated himself as he reviewed his cherished moments of butchery.

"That was the biggest kick in my life," he said, after he observed the tapes.

Armin had achieved the first stage of his fantasy. He had slaughtered a willing victim. Now he was ready to honor his chosen sacrifice by devouring him and absorbing his wisdom.

19

I Hope
I Won't
Be Lonely
Anymore

It was two days after Bernd's death. His flesh was ready to be eaten after being bled and hung, the meat now tender to cut. Armin spread the washed and ironed tablecloth over the dinner table. He fetched two china plates from his mother's dinner service in an overhead cupboard, and his best cutlery from the kitchen drawer. He gave them a quick wipe to get rid of the dust, then carefully laid the plates and cutlery in their correct positions on the table before neatly folding a white table napkin next to his place setting. He decorated the table with candles to set an intimate ambience. A vase of flowers added a romantic touch. He pondered bringing in the radio so he could listen to some classical music while he ate, but decided against it.

He wanted to focus purely on the food.

This was going to be the most important meal of his life. He was about to sample his first taste of human meat. He had carefully selected a particularly choice cut from

Bernd's body for dinner. It lay on the kitchen table now, waiting to be prepared. He had already deliberated with himself for hours about just what to cook for this meal. He finally decided on a big, bloody steak; it was a meal he knew he could sink his teeth into and really chew properly. He would use a recipe that he'd found on an internet cannibal forum; it was one meant to be particularly suitable for human flesh. This pleased him, as he didn't want to be too experimental with his first meal. He could afford to be more adventurous later on.

Armin laid out all the cooking ingredients on the chopping board. He had waxy new potatoes and Italian porcini mushrooms, as well as brussels sprouts and seasoning. He started to peel and slice the potatoes and mushrooms and chop up the garlic into thin pieces. When it came time to prepare the meat, he fondled the bloody steak, thrilled by the feeling of the raw flesh. Then he washed it under cold water and patted it dry with a piece of kitchen towel before tenderizing it with a rolling pin. He enjoyed pummeling the wooden instrument into the flesh—he could almost imagine the bluish bruises that would have formed on Bernd's skin had he still been alive.

Armin poured a generous helping of extra pure virgin olive oil into a frying pan and added the diced garlic and a pinch of nutmeg. He tenderly held the thick steak of Bernd's flesh in his hands before throwing it into the pan. The fat sizzled and spat as the meat hit the hot surface and started to soak up the olive oil. Armin breathed in deeply, and his nostrils caught the first aroma of cooked human meat.

He turned down the heat on the stove to a lower setting. He had learned earlier in the week, when they had tried to fry Bernd's penis, how easily human flesh could burn.

However impatient he was to taste his first mouthful of young male flesh, he didn't want to ruin *this* meal. All good things are worth waiting for, he told himself. He just needed a bit of patience.

He added the peeled brussels sprouts and new potatoes to a pan of boiling water. Then he scattered a handful of porcini mushrooms in the frying pan. They would go well with the garlic, he thought. He crushed peppercorns and added them to the pan to start a pepper sauce. He seared and turned the steak, then seared it again.

While the steak sizzled away, Armin washed and polished a crystal wineglass. He had opened a bottle of South African red wine earlier to let it breathe. The blood-red Merlot would be a perfect accompaniment to his meal. He turned over the sizzling meat in the frying pan once again. Juices oozed out of the steak as it cooked. The kitchen was filled with the savory smell of meat, and Armin's mouth watered as he imagined how sweet and tender the flesh would taste.

He turned off the heat. The steak was now medium rare, just to his liking. He always liked his steak served raw enough to make it easy for him to imagine it as part of an animal's flank. He wanted to be reminded of the steak's origins, not forget about them like so many other meat eaters.

He set the steak on a plate he had warmed in the oven, then garnished it with pepper sauce before adding the boiled vegetables.

"Dinner is served, at last," he said. "You certainly look good enough to eat now, Bernd."

He smoothed down his trousers, adjusted his tie and placed the napkin in his lap as he sat down at the table. He had waited all his life for his first taste of human meat; in just a few moments, he would eat it for the first time. He

decided to say a blessing first, a simple prayer he had
learned as a child.

> *"Thank you for the world so sweet,*
> *Thank you for the food we eat,*
> *Thank you for the birds that sing,*
> *Thank you God for everything.*
> *Amen."*

He added a few words of his own to the end of the
prayer:

> *"Lord God, thank you for this dinner and for providing me*
> *with food when I know that many on this earth are walking*
> *hungry. I hope that this meal will feed my body and nour-*
> *ish my soul. Thank you for providing me with a friend for*
> *life and for sacrificing Bernd's life on earth for me. I hope*
> *I won't be lonely anymore.*
> *Amen."*

He picked up his knife and sliced off a piece of the steak
before him. He looked at the shades of browns, reds and
pinks coloring the flesh. It was done to perfection. He cere-
moniously lifted his fork to his mouth and took his first bite.

He could still taste human blood as he chewed thought-
fully. The meat was warm and delicious and melted in his
mouth. It tasted just like pork. He had read that pigs were
closely related to humans, which could explain the similar
taste. He was thinking of Bernd's face when he had kissed
him last. "Finally I'm eating a strong, young male body,"
he said to Bernd's severed head, which he had placed beside him on the dinner table. "This is the most tasty meat
I've ever had. Nothing is so delicious!"

He chewed and swallowed and felt the meat pass
through his mouth and sink to his stomach. Bernd was in-

side him. Bernd could now join him in his body and soul with each mouthful that he took. Armin had no need to be on his own anymore. However solitary his daily pursuits, Bernd would always be with him. He may once have felt inadequate, or inferior, in his daily life, but this now made him feel godlike. It no longer mattered how all the boys had ribbed him at school for his strange clothes and habits, and ignored him socially. All the lonely evenings when he wished he had a friend were behind him now. He was a cannibal, or to use the Greek term, an *anthropophagus,* a *killer,* now. He had acted out his darkest thoughts and literally consumed another human. He was *powerful*.

Armin looked at the remaining flesh on his plate. Now that he had eaten his first mouthful, there would be no stopping him. He started slicing off large pieces of meat with his knife and biting very hard, chewing until the meat surrendered all its rich flavors. His memory of his dead friend strengthened with each mouthful that he swallowed. As he had hoped, Bernd's flesh was rich, superbly juicy and tender. Armin was in rapture each time he swallowed. "I've never eaten anything half as good as this," he said with relish. "This is the best meal I've ever had," he said out loud to Bernd's head. The sensation of consuming flesh was intensely erotic. The more he consumed, the more alive he felt. He experienced such sexual satisfaction as he swallowed and chewed, he thought he would attain an orgasm. He was panting with sexual tension by the time he had swallowed the last morsel of flesh. He then used a slice of bread to mop up his plate, so as not to waste any of the human juices.

He sat back as he finished his meal. He knew that cannibalism shocked and disgusted many, if not most, people. He was aware that what he had done was wrong—at least in society's eyes. He was conscious that he had taken a life and that Bernd would be missed among his family, friends and loved ones. On the other hand, he felt that the consumption of Bernd had completed him and given him a soul mate. "I can feel you with me again, dear Bernd," he said. "With every piece of flesh I ate, I remembered you."

Armin was convinced devouring Bernd had brought him closer to his former lover; he also believed he absorbed Bernd's skills, attributes and character when he digested his physical remains. He felt stronger, more intelligent and more versed in the ways of the world now, thanks to Bernd. He felt that Bernd had passed on his skills at speaking English, a language Armin had wanted to excel at but had done poorly at in school. His colleagues and neighbors didn't notice any changes in him, however.

He also believed there was a quasi-religious component to his actions. He reflected how Christians celebrate a metaphorical consumption of the Savior's body and blood in Holy Communion. He thought about how Jesus Christ symbolically underlined the primal custom of human sacrifice when he dined with his disciples at the Last Supper, urging them to "Take, eat: this is my body which is given for you." Armin had been taught as a child in the Roman Catholic Church that transubstantiation takes place during communion: the bread and wine actually *turn into* Christ's body and blood.

With this meal, he had attained his life's goal.

He could hardly wait for his next one.

In the following hours, Armin fasted as he eagerly searched online for recipes and even glanced through his mother's old cookbooks for inspiration. He wanted to prepare all sorts of meals from Bernd, and he wanted to cook him in every way possible, barbecuing some parts and following gourmet recipes for others.

At last he decided the next day's menu: "Ultra Succulent Pot Roast Dinner."

Once again he had found the winning recipe on a cannibal Web site.

For this meal, Armin rolled a piece of flesh in flour, sprinkled it with salt and pepper and rubbed on some garlic. Then he lightly seared the flesh in a large skillet before roasting it at a high temperature in the oven.

Over the next few months Armin ate almost half of his victim, defrosting the body parts piece by piece before consuming them. He cooked pieces of Bernd for all of his meals: he ate some along with his morning eggs, he made some into meatballs and brought them into work for lunch, and in the evenings he would cook dinners that he would eat alone, at home.

Never much of a chef until now, Armin grew confident in his kitchen skills as the weeks went by. He added to his growing collection of cannibal recipes, a collection that he had started earlier, and which included dishes called "Breaded Young Man's Liver" and "Bicep Cutlets in Port Wine Sauce." He often washed down his meals with a bottle of Muscat or a red South African Cabernet. He didn't invite anyone over to dinner to share his special meat, nor did he offer his colleagues any of the meatballs he took to the office; he wanted the flesh for himself. But Armin's hunger for human flesh wasn't abated by his numerous meals.

He continued to advertise for other victims as he ate his way through Bernd.

20

Bernd's Absence Is Noticed

The sky was darkening as night closed in on the city of Berlin on the evening of March 9, 2001. Bernd normally got home from the office at about 7:30 P.M.; he often left earlier on a Friday. Even on the rare occasions that he went out for a drink with his colleagues, he would be home by 9 P.M., so that he and his partner, Rene, could eat dinner together. It was now 9:45 P.M. and he was not at his apartment.

Rene racked his brain: had Bernd mentioned any meeting, conference or business trip? His partner always phoned to tell him if he was going to be late—he was very good like that. Rene checked the answering machine again. A mechanical voice told him he had "no messages." He pressed the button a second time and heard the same response. He turned his cell phone off and on to make sure it was working properly. The screen told him the battery was full and the message inbox was empty.

No one had tried to call him.

Rene felt irritated and let down.

Bernd had probably bumped into some friends on his way home and was no doubt having a thoroughly enjoyable evening, chatting over a beer or two in some bar. *He could have called me at least*, Rene thought, resentfully. *Then I could have joined him.* It was unfair of Bernd to leave him out, without even bothering to phone. Rene had gone to the supermarket to pick up the makings of their supper. He had bought a bottle of wine and the ingredients for a goat's cheese salad. He sullenly cut off a few slices of cheese. He was hungry and didn't want to wait any longer before eating. Bernd could fix himself a snack when he came home, Rene told himself. He wasn't going to bother cooking something for him now.

Rene poured himself a generous glass of wine and curled up on the couch. He turned on the TV and let an inane talk show entertain him for an hour or so. It looked like Bernd was going to be home late, and he wasn't prepared to wait up for him, so he turned in.

Rene woke up refreshed. He rolled over dozily, ready to snuggle into Bernd's back and nestle in the warmth of his body. But there was just a cold space on the other side of the mattress. Rene stretched and got out of bed.

"Morning, Bernd. What are you up to? Fancy some breakfast?" he said, stifling a yawn. He put on his slippers and plodded through to the kitchen. Bernd wasn't there. Nor was he in the living room. Rene wandered through to the study and checked in the bathroom. Also empty.

Perhaps Bernd slipped out to the bakery to buy some croissants for breakfast? Rene made himself some coffee and settled down in the kitchen chair. As he sipped his coffee, he remembered Bernd's late night out. He hadn't heard him come in. That wasn't very unusual. Rene was quite used to getting up and going to bed at different times than Bernd, and he could sleep through a good deal of noise. Still, he wondered why Bernd had gotten up so early if he had gone to bed so late. Could it be possible that Bernd hadn't come home at all?

Rene went back to their bedroom and really looked at their bed. It certainly didn't *look* slept in on Bernd's side. Bernd usually tangled up the duvet and sheets as he kicked his legs out in his dreams. Rene quickly looked in the wardrobe. Bernd's workday jacket and a pair of his shoes were missing. Rene felt worry tighten his stomach.

Something was wrong.

Rene forced himself to list justifiable excuses for Bernd's absence. His first thought was that Bernd had been to an all-night party and had crashed on someone's sofa or floor. But the truth was Bernd wasn't really up to wild parties anymore; he much preferred a night in front of the TV. Rene's mind then unearthed his worst insecurity: Bernd had met someone. He had left him for another man. Fear chilled his bones. Could this be true? Rene reflected on the past few months and had to conclude that the two of them had been happy. In fact, they had been going through a particularly good phase in their relationship. There was the occasional argument, but surely he would have known if Bernd had been having an affair. Bernd may have been an introvert, but he would have given at least some signs if he was in love with someone else, wouldn't he? *Unless* leaving suddenly was Bernd's way of exiting their relationship without having to experience recriminations or bitter tears . . .

Rene banished all thoughts of infidelity out of his mind. He decided he was overreacting and being silly. Bernd would never want to hurt him. Rene had to trust him. He took a shower and went shopping. He spent that Saturday afternoon with friends, and reassured himself that Bernd would be home soon, with an explanation involving some mishap or a funny story.

But Rene came home to an empty flat that night.

He started to worry anew. He called a few mutual friends and tried to keep his tone casual as he asked them whether they had heard from Bernd. No one had heard from him for days, he was told. Rene decided not to phone Bernd's father just yet; he doubted Bernd was at his dad's. Theirs wasn't a close relationship.

By Monday morning, Rene felt an edge of panic.

He *still* hadn't heard anything from Bernd. Friends told him not to worry, but Rene couldn't understand why Bernd hadn't been in touch. It just wasn't like him. He was scared. His mind kept on returning to his uppermost fear: Bernd had left him for another man. Or even another woman. He knew about Bernd's checkered sexual history; he had even met some of Bernd's ex girlfriends. Rene now grew increasingly upset with each additional hour that passed.

He decided to call Bernd at work. He knew he shouldn't disturb him there, Bernd's colleagues didn't know about their relationship, or even that Bernd was gay. But if he could just *talk* to Bernd, maybe everything would be all right. His heart pounded hard as he dialed Bernd's office number. The number rang a few times and then clicked into answering machine mode. Rene had resolved to leave a calm message, but hearing Bernd's voice on the machine stirred up his emotions. He left a desperate message, one that conveyed all his misery: "Bernd, it's Rene here. I need to talk to you. I'm worried. Please come home. Whatever has happened, I'm sure we can work it out. Just come home, please."

Bernd's colleagues had yet to share Rene's concern; they hadn't paid much attention when he didn't turn up for work that morning. It wasn't unusual for a colleague to be late. "He probably has a doctor or a dentist appointment or something, and forgot to tell us about it," Stefan Pommerening told another colleague. "Or maybe he's ill, has come down with some flu bug."

His colleagues didn't start to wonder where Bernd was until they went for lunch. They missed Bernd's jokes and wanted to find out about his weekend in London. So Stefan checked his colleague's answering machine for messages. He listened to Rene's voice, sounding very miserable, asking Bernd to come home, and was surprised by the emotion he heard. It wasn't the type of message you'd expect from a roommate. He wondered if Bernd was homosexual. He knew Bernd shared an apartment with another man, but he had never considered them a couple. He was confused. Bernd had spent many afternoons bragging about his sexual exploits with various women—he had never indicated that he was anything but heterosexual.

Stefan didn't call Rene back.

He didn't know what to say. He had no idea why Bernd wasn't at work, but he was sure there was probably a mundane reason behind his disappearance. Besides, he didn't want to get involved in some sort of romantic drama or domestic dispute.

Rene wondered why Bernd hadn't picked up his phone. He tried the number again, but got the same answering machine message. His fears moved to deeper level. What if Bernd hadn't gone to work either? What if he had been in an accident or had hurt himself? He could have been attacked on his way home, even! Panic swept over him as he registered the range of sinister possibilities that could be behind the disappearance. Berlin was a big city, and all kinds of crime inhabited its urban streets.

Bernd's manager called the flat later that Monday afternoon to inquire if Bernd was sick or if there was another reason why he hadn't turned up for work. The phone call deepened Rene's sense of panic. He decided to get in touch with the police to register Bernd as missing.

The police were polite but not overly concerned. They received enough calls about missing people to know that many were caused by relationship breakdowns, extramarital affairs or simple domestic squabbles. And Bernd had only been missing a weekend. It hardly gave them immediate cause for alarm. Rene informed the police that Bernd was also missing from work. He felt frustrated by their lack of concern.

That evening, Rene turned over the flat to hunt for an explanation or clue for Bernd's absence. He searched through Bernd's coat pockets for unusual receipts and sniffed his shirts to catch any whiff of a stranger's aftershave. Jealousy drove him to try and hack into Bernd's e-mail account, but he couldn't come up with the right password. He looked through Bernd's files on the computer and was surprised to see nothing but empty folders on the hard drive. Rene finally searched through the papers in the study. At first all he found were routine bills and receipts. Then he noticed a thick sealed envelope, with his name on the front, beneath the desk. He tore open the envelope, expecting a long emotional farewell letter.

Instead he found Bernd's will.

His hands started to shake.

What on earth did this mean? Was Bernd contemplating suicide? Rene read through the contents of Bernd's last will and testament and learned Bernd had left most of his estate to him. He flicked through the lengthy document and shook out the pages, hoping to find some personal note addressed to him between the sheets. Bernd couldn't have committed suicide, he told himself. Surely he would have left a farewell letter or said goodbye. He wouldn't simply vanish. It just didn't make any sense. . . .

He called the police again first thing the next morning, but for the second time, they failed to reassure him. The police told him Bernd would probably come home that day, and to try not to worry. In the meantime, they would start their own investigation. Rene was now desperate, and decided to take matters into his own hands. At random, he contacted Nina Hermann, a former journalist at the *Berliner Zeitung*, a city newspaper. He hoped her investigative skills would solve the mystery of Bernd's disappearance.

After listening to Rene's story, Nina agreed to help. A reporter able to assess the situation objectively—unlike Rene, whose emotions were on edge—she suspected that something had happened to Bernd. However, she tried to conceal her worries until she had hard evidence. She got in touch with Bernd's bank and found out there was no outgoing activity on his account since a few days before his disappearance, so she was able to rule out that Bernd had deserted Rene and his life in Berlin. She also ruled out the possibility that Bernd had left Rene to pursue a relationship with someone else. Bernd would need cash to do either thing.

She then called up Bernd's and Rene's friends and acquaintances. None of them had heard anything from Bernd, or seen him since the previous weekend, apart from a colleague of Bernd's, who had spotted him at Berlin's main railway station on the day of his disappearance. Bernd hadn't noticed him. With this small lead, Rene and Nina immediately went down to the station and looked around for evidence pointing to what had happened. They talked to the station officials and people working in the shops and food stalls, but nobody could remember anything out of the ordinary, or a man fitting Bernd's description. They searched for possible suicide sites near the station area—a bridge Bernd might have jumped off, or anything obvious. Nothing was apparent, and station officials would have reported it if a man had killed himself by throwing his body on the tracks. They realized that Bernd could have taken a train somewhere, but Rene had no idea *where*.

They published a photo of Bernd in the paper after he had been missing for a week. Bernd's colleagues were shocked to see it. They had no idea where he might have gone, or what might have happened to him. After several weeks there weren't any responses with useful information as to Bernd's whereabouts. The police hadn't discovered any clues either, and after speaking to his employers, family and friends, they declared the case closed.

Rene's heart was broken.

How could no one know where had Bernd disappeared to?

Of course, there was one person who knew where Bernd had gone that day, but he wasn't likely to tell anyone. He had already eaten a lot of the evidence.

21

Looking for Another Slaughter Boy

The wives of Wüstefeld had been busy baking cakes, each eager to outshine the other with their creations of chocolate, icing, sugar and cream. The village was holding its summer garden party, and seventy to eighty people had been invited. They had been promised a good spread of food, and the women didn't want to disappoint them. On a long wooden table they arranged plates of cold meats, sausages and cheese next to bowls of potato salad and loaves of fresh bread. The cakes and desserts were honored with a separate table. The villagers enjoyed these regular get-togethers, and made the most of the social occasion.

Armin stood in the shade, away from the chattering groups of friends, and nibbled on a sandwich he had assembled out of slices of pork and a crusty white roll. The meat tasted bland to him; over the last few months he had grown accustomed to the taste of human flesh, and the tame, manufactured taste of chemically treated pork disappointed him.

He felt awkward—he never felt at ease in this sort of social setting.

He approached a group of neighbors and made an attempt at conversation. Nobody noticed anything new about him that day, or indeed had noticed anything different about him during the previous months. Despite Armin's belief that eating Bernd had given him some of his victim's personality and abilities, to the neighbors he was unchanged, still the somewhat strange but harmless man who lived in the ancient farmhouse down the road. They would never have guessed a killer lurked in their midst, or that a pile of human bones lay buried in their odd neighbor's backyard. A quarter of a year had passed since Armin had killed Bernd, and in all that time Armin had kept up normal appearances to the outside world. He continued to work hard and be civil to his colleagues. He helped cook the hamburgers at the village barbecues, though he never supplied the meat, human or otherwise.

But Armin *had* changed; he was a real cannibal now, not a pretend one.

His guard slipped once, during a night out with a former school friend. Alcohol had loosened his tongue, and he told his friend he was in Internet contact with a man "who is always asking me whether he is ripe for slaughter." The friend was baffled. What on earth was he talking about? As soon as Armin sobered up, he realized his mistake and asked his friend to forget about the conversation. His friend duly dismissed the comments as mere drunken ramblings; he believed Armin had spent too many hours playing violent computer games that had sparked his imagination.

So Armin got away with some careless words.

But he was growing restless.

His obsession with cannibalism hadn't waned; the taste of Bernd's flesh hadn't sated his appetite for human flesh. On the contrary, it had made him hungry for more. He had already consumed two-thirds of his victim's flesh and he was eager to replenish his freezer. After five months of silence, Franky had logged back on to cannibal newsgroups in search of a new victim. There were at least eight-hundred active participants in the cannibal forums, and he was confident he could find men for new meals among them. He chatted online almost daily with like-minded people, in chat rooms and forums with names such as Gourmet, Cannibal Cafe and Eaten Up.

"I hope to find another victim soon because flesh is everything," Armin told a fellow fanatic in an e-mail.

He also placed another series of online ads—after all, they had worked the first time.

One read: "Looking for a well-built, nice young man, between 18 and 25, for a real slaughter and feast. Please apply with statistics, including age, height and weight, if possible with a photo." Another read: "Slaughter boy sought. Are you between 18 and 25 years old, healthy and with a normal build? Do you want to end your life, but you want something decent to come out of you, then come to me. I will slaughter you and worship your body, in delicious schnitzel and steaks. Those interested, should apply with details of age, height and weight, ideally with a photo. Franky, the master butcher."

Armin was confident enough now to call himself a "master butcher." He had butchered a human; he wasn't an amateur anymore.

He continued his online hunt for tender, young flesh. With his fellow cannibal addicts, he played with the uncertainties implicit in the posted offers of killing and dying that were on the cannibal forums. Chat-room participants from different countries and continents experienced thrills as they tried to guess whether the people who posted their messages meant their words of death for real—or, indeed, how far to the edge they themselves were prepared to go. Armin's interest was finally attracted by an ad from *eatmefordinner@hotmail.com*. The advertisement read: "I am a 25-year-old male based in London looking for someone to devour me piece by piece. I'm not interested in talking to anyone who's not serious about eating me. I mean it. I have a sporty physique and am six foot two." Armin also liked the sound of "Manntoll," who told readers in his broken English, "I am search a human-butcher, for me, i will in the year 2004 butchered, you can me splitt, cut and eat, alive."

But neither *eatmefordinner@hotmail.com* or Manntoll would agree to meet for a romantic dinner date.

Armin lowered his requirements. He placed another ad as Franky, this one declaring that his victim could be as old as thirty years, with a "normal built body." Despite Armin's belief that his English had improved since eating Bernd, the ad read, in part: "I will butchering you and eating your fine flesh." A "Hänsi" saw the ad, and got in touch; "Dear Franky, I have been looking for an experienced butcher for a long time, who will stun me like a bull and will then let me bleed to death. When are you going to bleed me?"

Armin replied immediately: "Hänsi, please get in touch, I'm a very hungry cannibal and can hardly wait to meet. Please email me your exact stats."

Franky got the answer he wanted: "Franky, I'm 178 cm tall, 78kg naked, with black hair, a strong physique and I am healthy. When do you plan my slaughter date?"

Armin asked Hänsi for a direct e-mail, so they could leave the posting board, chat privately, and "sort out details, meeting point, time." He told him he would "expertly slaughter and chop him up" and completely devour him. Signing himself off as Franky, Armin wrote, "I'm already really looking forward to slaughtering you and dining on your delicious flesh." Hänsi never wrote in the forum again.

Like many other chat-room participants, for all his big words, he didn't really mean it.

He was just playing.

Armin was frustrated by his lack of progress. He thought back to Jörg, a thirty-two-year-old cook from Villingen Schwenningen in southern Germany, whom he'd gotten to know in July 2000, prior to Bernd's slaughter. Jörg had also lost the courage to be cannibalized. And they had come so close! The cook, who had a pointy nose and goatee beard, initially offered up his colleagues as potential meals before agreeing to meet Armin at his Rotenburg farmhouse to play slaughter games. Armin had tied Jörg up and marked out choice bits on his body with a pen before stringing him up on a meat hook. The cook had complained that his ankles hurt, and Armin let him down. Jörg left the farmhouse soon after, saying he felt queasy.

Armin gazed at his two naked pictures of Bernd. There, at least, was someone who had acted on his promise, and had gone through with it, right to the end. Surely there was another Bernd out there for him.

Although Armin was able to lure more slaughter boys to his home—his ads turned up four men who initially agreed to become his supper—none ever made it to his dinner table. The four men, one from London and the others from the German cities of Kassel, Essen and Odenwald near Frankfurt, all agreed to come to Armin's house to indulge in their dark sexual fantasies.

When Stefan, a teacher from nearby Kassel, responded to Franky's online ad, Armin reassured him that he wasn't deterred by Stefan's age. "Being 30 is certainly in a suitable slaughter age," he wrote. When Stefan arrived at the farmhouse, Armin stripped him naked, laid him on the slaughter bench and wrapped him up in cellophane. He stuck needles with paper labels into Stefan's skin, marking the most succulent pieces of Stefan with the words "ham" or "fillet." But Stefan found it "too cold" when Armin hung him on the meat hook, so he was cut down. The two men had pizza for dinner, then Stefan went home.

Another prospective meal turned up from the German city of Essen. Armin led his new playmate to the slaughter room, where he wrapped him in cellophane. The victim begged Armin to lock him in the wooden cage in the butchery; Armin obliged him. Then he demanded to be fed like an animal. The victim grunted and squealed like a trapped pig for about an hour as Armin threw him scraps of pig's bacon and pieces of bread. The man hungrily gobbled up the food without using his hands, as he crawled around on all fours like an animal. But this man also didn't want to be killed. He said he got excited by *simulating* death—not by the real thing. Armin let him go.

Armin could have killed either of these men as they lay on the slaughter bench or were strung up from the hook. They had no chance of freeing themselves. But he untied them and let them go. It was important for him to know he wasn't a depraved serial killer; he was a *cannibal* who only wanted to slaughter a man who was willing.

A third man, called Alex, from Odenwald, paid a visit to Armin's slaughter room and pushed Armin to decapitate him. But Armin refused—he found the young man to be too stupid and too fat in person to be worthy of slaughter. He was a cannibal, but he was also selective in his choice of victims.

The same applied in the case of Daniel, whom Armin also found too fat. They met online and Daniel sent a photo. Armin's ideal type was still slim and blond—after eating Bernd, he was a fussy eater who only wanted lean, choice cuts. He turned down one other candidate he met online, a man who wanted his genitals burned by a flamethrower. That was a bit too strange—Armin wasn't interested in anyone "weird."

Finally, some six months after Bernd was killed and butchered, Armin's ad was seen by Dirk. They made contact, and Dirk flew over from London, to meet in person. He worked as an event manager and conference organizer for an international hotel chain, and had previously worked abroad, in Saudi Arabia and Switzerland. Armin was impressed by Dirk's travels and thought him worldly-wise— but it was a shy man with black, spiky gelled hair that turned up at Armin's house.

Armin ran his eyes over Dirk's thin frame and hollow shoulders. He could do with a bit more meat on his bones, but he would serve as a second victim. Also, Dirk was only twenty-seven years old, a suitable slaughter age, which pleased Armin. This slaughter boy's meat should still be quite fresh.

The two chatted and got to know each other. Armin had been through all of this before, and felt he knew what to expect. This time he wanted to get down to business and avoid too much procrastination, so after a short conversation to put his potential victim at ease, he led Dirk up to the slaughter room and proudly showed off his handiwork. Dirk was delighted as he gazed around the room.

"This is impressive," he said. "It's a real death chamber."

Dirk liked talking about corpses and anything to do with dying, he confessed. Death was his biggest turn-on. Armin quickly assured his guest that talking about death was something he could happily arrange.

"This is so exciting, really erotic," Dirk continued.

"What I want is to be sentenced to death. Would you do that for me?"

"Sure," Armin replied. "Your death penalty is coming up!"

He ran downstairs, happy to oblige his victim's last wishes. He turned on his computer, tapped away on his keyboard and dutifully printed out a death sentence. Dirk's face lit up as he read through it. He noticed the time of death was due in an hour, and lots of torture was promised. Talking and thinking about death aroused him. He felt his body grow hot.

"Do you like it?" Armin asked.

"It's perfect," Dirk replied. "I want to be chained so I can't escape. I'll be at your mercy."

Armin chained Dirk to the metal frame of the bed in the makeshift abattoir. Dirk was stripped naked and wrapped in cellophane. Armin stuck pins in his body, indicating his liver, kidney and other organs. They agreed these were to be cut out for consumption. Armin was getting excited. He had *finally* gotten his hands on a second victim! He decided to taunt Dirk a little. He was enjoying the feeling of power. He dangled a photo of Jörg Boese in front of Dirk's face. He showed him more photos of Jörg stripped naked and hanging upside down and watched Dirk's face grow pale.

Dirk was scared. He didn't want to go *that* far. His fantasies to be killed and butchered quickly evaporated. "I don't want to go through with it," he blurted. "I want to go home."

Armin froze. How could Dirk back out at the last minute and change his mind like that? How disappointing, how *inconsiderate*.

"Get me out of this now," Dirk started to panic.

Armin didn't move.

"Unchain me. I want to go home!"

Armin reminded himself he only wanted a totally consensual victim. With regret, he released Dirk from his chains of death. After he had said goodbye, a mood of dark depression sank over him. None of the slaughter boys he found seemed willing to be eaten. He was filled with despair, because Bernd wasn't enough.

He was ready now to kill somebody else.

22

Franky Boasts

Self-confidence was a novel sensation for Armin, but it was one he now wore gladly. He had something to be proud of. He had eaten someone; he was a cannibal with a man's blood between his teeth, and he liked the taste. There was only one problem—he had no one to share his achievement with. Bernd, of course, had witnessed some of the savage act, and that knowledge gave him great satisfaction. He was conscious, though, that he needed to tread carefully elsewhere; common sense told him to hide his moment of glory, conceal his life's triumph from the world's uncomprehending eyes, much as it pained him.

But as the months passed, the urge to brag grew.

He needed to boast of his victory, and of his transformation into a superior being.

Finally, the urge to share his deeds taunted him until he couldn't stand it any longer. He decided that if he couldn't reveal his deadly secret to the world, he could at least tell a tiny portion of it. And he knew exactly where he could find an appreciative audience. He settled into his habitual evening pose, slumped in a chair behind one of his computers, and scrolled his mouse over to the icon that would connect him to the Internet, and to the online world of cannibalism. His chat-room friends understood a cannibal's drives and his passions. They would surely recognize his achievement in killing and eating a man.

Armin logged on to a chat-room forum as Franky and boasted that he had killed a man and eaten him—Franky, the master butcher, had actually gone ahead and done it. And, he added, he had done a fine, professional job of massacring the victim's body and serving it up as steaks. Once he started revealing his secrets, he found it difficult to stop. He logged on to other cannibal forums and boasted there too. It felt so good to let it all pour out and feel that someone was *listening*. Yet he wasn't satisfied with mere words; they didn't do full justice to the slaughter. He wanted to illustrate his acts; he decided to publish the photos he had taken of his potential victims. He wanted people online to admire the slaughter scenes he had acted out with them, and see some of his majestic work, even if they couldn't see the slaughter of Bernd. In this way he could finally bask in the limelight. Once the pictures were posted, Armin warmed with the sensation of imaginary applause from a crowd of ardent fans, and took a sweeping bow to an empty room.

All of this online bragging soon drew attention among cannibal wannabes.

Chat-room participants had to admit that this man Franky was really convincing—it *almost* sounded as if he really had gone ahead and acted out their shared dream, even if few among them would truly have killed and eaten a man, or allowed someone to kill and eat them, even if given the opportunity. Cannibalism was the fodder of their *fantasy;* they didn't want to be part of a horrific sex murder; they just wanted to play a game.

On July 9, 2001, a university student in the Austrian city of Innsbruck came across Franky's outspoken ads and boastful postings while he was chatting online. He read them with amazement. The student was intrigued as he scrolled through the cannibal Web pages; cannibalism wasn't his favored fantasy, but it held a macabre fascination for him. He wanted to surf the sites to find out more. The destructive and aggressive sexual fantasies that flew back and forth between the chat-room participants aroused his curiosity. He couldn't believe the way some of them wallowed voluntarily in such self-degradation. He was young and interested in the bizarre, and he wanted to delve into this sinister world and discover more about it, experience some of it for himself. He typed in a message to Franky, and the two chatted about cannibalism. Then the Austrian student offered himself up for slaughter, curious whether he could provoke a reaction.

Franky replied quickly—yes, he would be interested in the student for dinner. The student's written promises were giving Armin an appetite, he wrote. He also pointed out that the fact that the student was young meant soft, juicy tenderloin steaks.

When the student opened Franky's reply, he gasped out loud. His stomach turned as he realized that Franky was serious about looking for someone to slaughter. It wasn't just role-play. He recoiled in horror as he read through the words of a killer, live on his computer screen. The student felt increasingly nauseous as he registered that Franky had *already* killed someone. And what's more, he was out there right now seeking additional victims on the Internet!

The student was terrified.

He was scared that this Franky could trace him now that he had his e-mail address.

He quickly deleted his Lycos e-mail account and his on-line personal details. He didn't want Franky to be able to get in touch with him ever again, and he certainly didn't want him to find out where he lived. He shut down his computer. That didn't feel like enough, so he also pulled out the plug. He wanted to rid himself of the irrational fear that Franky could somehow see him through the computer screen. He tried to calm his nerves, and he had one clear thought: *I've got to do something about this; this man is dangerous.*

However, he didn't want to confide in his friends; it would be too embarrassing. He was concerned that they would consider him a sexual deviant and weird for having contacted Franky in the first place. And talking to university professors was definitely a bad idea—he didn't want to be thrown off his degree course for misconduct, or smudge his clean reputation in any way. But it was important that the authorities be alerted about this killer on the loose. He decided he would have to go to the police.

With his heart in his mouth, he dialed the number of the Federal Criminal Police Office in Wiesbaden, the capital of the German state of Hesse. He told the police everything that had happened, and helped all he could with their inquiries. But that was as far as the student was prepared to go. He stressed to the police that he was keen to remain anonymous, and that he wasn't prepared to appear in any court case. He still felt a chill run down his spine every time he thought about how he'd danced with death by corresponding with a killer. Now all he wished to do was forget the world of cannibalism. He wanted to wash his hands free of the episode and return to his studies with a clean conscience.

The police thanked the university student for his tip-off and said they would follow it up.

After this student came forward, Franky attracted additional readers in the cannibal forums—undercover officers. Following the student's lead, they accessed the online world of cannibalism and answered Armin's ad. The police specialists quickly determined that Franky meant his ad literally. They weren't yet sure if they were dealing with an evil psychopath, a mentally disturbed liar or a genuine killer, but they were determined to find out more.

Two months later, the police identified Franky as Armin Meiwes.

23

Have
You
Eaten
Human Flesh,
Mr. Meiwes?

It was shortly before Christmas 2002. The snow was piling up on the roofs of the town of Rotenburg, as winter settled in. The charming architecture of the buildings, and the merry scenes in the Christmas markets—where one could buy Lebkuchen ginger cookies or mulled wine—painted an idyllic Christmas card scene.

The local children had celebrated St. Nikolaus' Day on December 6. The reverend gray-haired saint was said to have a flowing beard and to wear a bishop's garments, including a gold-embroidered cape, a miter and a pastoral staff. According to German tradition, the saint went from door to door on that particular evening and asked children if they had been good during the past twelve months. The children often performed a song or poem, or showed off some other such skill, to prove to St. Nikolaus that they were worthy and obedient little boys and girls. Small gifts and chocolate figures were then distributed to those children who had been well behaved.

No one had knocked on Armin's door on St. Nikolaus' Day. He hadn't received any presents or candy to reward him for good behavior that year. Nor had he been able to show off his particular talents to anyone on the night of December 6. A few days later, on December 10, however, there was a persistent knocking on his front door. It was 8:45 A.M., an early hour for callers during the holiday season.

Armin opened his front door.

Standing there were three police officers.

He invited them in, and acted as if they were neighbors who had come round to share a festive slice of Christmas stollen. He asked the police if they would care for some coffee, and apologized for not having any Christmas ginger biscuits to offer. His impeccable manners did not fail him; he pulled back the chair for the female police officer as she sat down at the kitchen table. Armin joined them at the table, and his cool demeanor surprised the three officers. They observed that this alleged "cannibal" didn't seem panicked, guilt-ridden or even overly concerned by their visit. The mild-mannered man they were having coffee with seemed quite normal. They wondered if he really was a killer. They informed him that they weren't making a friendly neighborhood call. They told him that they had a warrant to search the house, following suspicions that he had murdered a man and eaten his body.

Armin was quiet as he registered the implications of their words. The police obviously knew something, but how much? There was always the possibility that they wouldn't find enough evidence to arrest him, and he certainly wasn't prepared to help them find it. He decided to keep his cards close to his chest. He calmly inquired on what grounds they were basing their suspicions, and who had made the allegations against him.

"You told us yourself in your messages on cannibal Web sites," a policeman bluntly replied.

The police began their questioning, and they were direct. "Have you eaten human flesh, Mr. Meiwes?"

"I may have," Armin enigmatically replied.

Armin's reply immediately made the police suspicious; the man they were questioning wasn't prepared to protest his innocence. It was also likely that, if guilty, Armin wasn't going to immediately confess his sins. His words *sounded* like those of a man who had something to hide; they needed to scour the property for any traces of murder, including the remnants of a body.

After questioning Armin for approximately twenty minutes, the police officers began their search of the old farmhouse that looked like nobody had cleaned or cared for it in years. Their first stop was the kitchen. Dirty dishes stood in the sink, left over from Armin's breakfast. There was a bread bin, a rack full of potatoes, a collection of various green vegetables and a cupboard full of tinned produce. A police officer flung open the fridge door, half expecting a gruesome corpse to fall out. A jar of mustard, a hunk of cheese and a carton of milk greeted him instead. The next appliance to be opened was the white cold-storage cabinet in the corner. The freezer unit was notably large; it looked like it could pack enough food for a sizable family, yet they knew from their earlier questioning that Armin Meiwes lived by himself. The police officers exchanged a quick glance before lifting up the freezer door and peering inside. There were neatly packed blue bags of something resembling meat arranged neatly inside.

An officer cautiously picked up one of the blue bundles. It was meat for sure. But they couldn't identify it as human flesh merely by looking at it. They delved deeper into the freezer and unearthed approximately twenty packages of blue freezer bags, all filled with meal-size portions of meat. The officers carefully unloaded the rest of the meat from the freezer. A frozen pizza was the only other food stored there. From the frost covering it, it seemed to have been around for a long while. The only other thing in the freezer was a dead rat. It had been flattened by the heavy packages of meat on top of it. The police left it alone.

The investigators looked through the pile of frozen packages in front of them. They were staring at what might be human flesh in the house of an alleged murderer and cannibal. The evidence seemed to speak for itself. But the meat *could* be pork, or that of another animal. They needed to take the flesh to a forensic laboratory to determine if it was indeed human before they could accuse Armin of any crime.

They continued their investigation of the house, looking for more evidence.

The next obvious place to search was the horde of computers in the dilapidated study. It was online activity that had led them to Armin in the first place. The detectives looked at the pile of computers, which were stacked up untidily, one on top of the other. What did he do with them all, and why did he need so many? Even for an IT worker, it seemed excessive. The detectives switched on the computers and scoured through Armin's documents. The private world where he had retreated most nights was now fully exposed to the probing eyes of the law. The police flicked through the numerous photos Armin had stored; they saw 3,842 pictures in all, illustrating a mixture of pornography, torture scenes and Armin's holiday snaps. The detectives were rapidly getting a sense of the type of man they were dealing with.

The police also discovered stacks of pornographic and masochistic videotapes during their two-and-a-half-hour

search of the house. The pictures of torment and purposefully inflicted pain on the tapes disturbed even the experienced professionals. The one tape they did *not* find was
Armin's favorite. He had hidden the video depicting
Bernd's slaughter months earlier to keep it safe from any
visitors.

As evidence, the police now had sixteen computers,
about two hundred hard drives and three hundred videos,
in addition to the frozen meat they had found. They continued their tour of the dust-filled rooms on the first floor,
which were cluttered with ancient furniture and old junk.
Then they made their way to the second floor. No one,
apart from Bernd and potential victims, had visited that
part of the house for two years. Armin grew noticeably nervous as he accompanied them upstairs. The police opened
the door to the makeshift slaughterhouse and wandered
through the rust-stained room, staring in disbelief. They
noted the trough drains, and the meat hooks that hung from
the ceiling. They were amazed as they looked at little
Minchen's killing knives, neatly laid out and arranged according to size on the slaughter table, and the life-size
mannequin that hung from a meat hook on the wall.

Evidence was mounting up against Armin. The police felt
that all signs indicated they were dealing with a severely disturbed individual—yet none proved he had actually murdered a man. While they awaited DNA analysis of the
meat, the only charge they could bring against him was
the "glorification of violence" following their discovery of
the violent videos and images in his home. The police officers had plenty of incriminating evidence, but as they took
their leave, Armin was still a free man.

He said goodbye to the police and shut his front door.
The law was sniffing around, trying to find out his secrets,
and he didn't know how long he could keep them hidden.
The police had just gathered vital clues to Bernd's death,

but they had missed the video showing the slaughter. And they didn't seem to know Bernd's name—they hadn't questioned him about Bernd's disappearance. He had been relaxed and amiable with the police, but he knew they were suspicious.

They were on his case.

He wasn't sure what he could do about it.

24

Listen,
I'm in
Trouble

Armin had been pacing the house for hours, trying to determine his next course of action, and he still didn't know what to do. He needed to confide in someone and ask for advice. The problem was he didn't know whom he could turn to. Who *can* you talk to, when you've eaten someone and are about to be found out? The local priest wasn't likely to lend a nonjudgmental, understanding ear. Armin eventually decided to telephone Ingbert, his brother who worked as an IT specialist in Frankfurt. He wasn't particularly close to his brother and his sister-in-law, but they were family and should be prepared to help him, or at least hear him out.

Armin dialed his brother's number. He could scarcely believe he was about to confess his anthropophagus acts to his own family, after years of carefully concealing his dark secrets. His sister-in-law answered the phone, and Armin was relieved. He knew he would confess his sins to her from the moment he heard her warm and friendly voice say, "Hello." A woman might be more understanding, and be prepared to offer some compassion. He knew what he wanted to say to her, but it was difficult to utter the words. After identifying himself, he cleared his voice several times, but failed to verbalize anything.

"Armin, are you still there?" his sister-in-law asked, after listening to a long silence.

"Yes, I'm still here," he managed, in a shaky voice. "Listen, I'm in trouble."

"What kind of trouble?" she asked. "Armin, tell me what's happened. Are you all right?"

Armin paused, then informed his sister-in-law that the police had turned up earlier that day and raided his home. "Look, I could be in serious trouble if they look on the hard drives of my computers," he said. "There are things there that they shouldn't see."

His sister-in-law's first suspicion was that Armin was involved with child pornography. She had often wondered about his sexuality, had always thought it strange her brother-in-law had failed to form a relationship with a woman, or indeed, with a man. She had never, however, considered him a pervert until this moment. She felt disgusted as she wondered if a member of her own family had been looking at sexual pictures of children. "Are you trying to tell me you've been looking at child pornography?" she questioned in clipped tones. "Is that why they've seized your computers?"

Armin's answer was even more shocking than she'd expected.

"I've killed someone," he told her bluntly.

Armin put down the receiver. His sister-in-law couldn't really help him. He felt better, though, for having unburdened himself a little. And now that he had calmed down, he realized that his options were limited. He could run away, but he didn't know to where. And besides, the police would catch up with him eventually. He wasn't stupid—he knew they would discover that the meat they had confiscated was human flesh once the forensic tests had been completed. He was about to be found out as a cannibal, and no elaborate lie could extricate him. The police were pursuing him, and he needed to act fast. And the only person who could help him, he decided, was his lawyer.

That afternoon, Armin drove to Rotenburg for an appointment with Harald Ermel, a local lawyer with a small practice, who dealt mainly with matrimonial law. Armin had hired Ermel once, when he had needed to sort out a drunk driving offense.

"I've done something stupid," Armin told Ermel.

The lawyer wondered what his client was about to tell him. Maybe Armin had been involved in a dispute with a neighbor over land? Or perhaps something had happened at work? There weren't many big legal cases in the peaceful town of Rotenburg at Christmastime, and he wasn't expecting one to land on his desk now.

"'I've killed and eaten someone,'" Armin confessed to Ermel.

The lawyer nearly fell off his chair.

Armin calmly added that he wanted some legal advice.

Ermel quickly pulled himself together, and assessed the situation. This ordinary-looking man seated opposite him, who had previously asked him about a driving license offense, had killed and eaten someone? His client was a self-confessed *cannibal* and he was asking him what he should do about it? The lawyer advised Armin to give himself up to the police. It was the only course of action. Armin realized he didn't have much choice, and agreed. Ermel contacted the police. He informed them that his client had just admitted he had killed a man and consumed the corpse.

The police immediately drove over and issued a warrant for Armin Meiwes's arrest.

Armin didn't resist his arrest; having discussed it with his lawyer he understood that any opposition was not only futile but could result in additional charges. He wanted to make the best of the situation. He was taken into custody and driven to the police station, where he made a statement, confessing to his crime at about 5 P.M. "I admit what I've done," he told the police in the statement. "I accept that I am guilty and I regret my actions." He immediately gave the police Bernd's name, to allow them to identify the victim.

Armin spent the night in a police cell.

The following morning, investigators returned to Armin's house to continue searching the property, this time taking sniffer dogs with them to hunt for evidence, a digger to excavate the grounds, and a hearse for Bernd's remains. Meanwhile, Armin was cooperative with the police. He showed them the chat rooms, which they would have had trouble accessing without his assistance, and helped them find the evidence they needed. He also told them about the bone meal he had ground out of Bernd's arm. Armin knew exactly what to do, so as not to portray himself in a bad light. His lawyer had advised him prior to his arrest to be cooperative, and he was intelligent enough to realize that this made sense.

Armin seemed to have few regrets; he seemed happy to be able to tell someone his story and divulge all of the gory details to the horrified police officers during a series of interviews. He admitted that he had videotaped himself killing Bernd, whom he had met via a gay Internet chat room, and who had responded to one of his eighty ads asking for slaughter boys.

Detective Wilfried Fehl was chosen to evaluate the
video of Bernd's slaughter. Fehl felt revolted as he watched
Armin saw off his victim's limbs and dissect his body into
meal-size portions. "It's practically unimaginable what he
did," Fehl later told colleagues. The videocassette fully il-
lustrated the nature of Bernd's death. With such disturbing
visual evidence available, the question now was not
whether Armin would be convicted or not, but on what
charge.

The detectives searched for further evidence in the
overgrown grounds of the sprawling seventeenth-century
estate. They examined the heap of old cars and the various
broken pieces of machinery and equipment that lay scattered around the untidy garden. They found nothing. They
located an electric saw, and a barbecue grill that looked
like it had been used recently, as it still had traces of fat on
it, and they confiscated them. Both could have been oper-
ated for alleged criminal purposes, they determined.

The sniffer dogs were particularly interested in one corner of the garden; they dragged their handlers over and
pawed frantically at the ground. The detectives noted that
someone had been digging in this part of the garden and
had disturbed the soil.

The detectives focused on this particular area for the
next stage of their investigation. They started up their
small digger and began tearing into the ground. The machine unearthed stones and trash, before its metal spade hit
against something hard. The investigators pulled the object
out of the ground. It was a large bone, and it looked human.
They carried on until they had unburied all of the remnants
of Bernd's decaying body—just bones remained. They had
the body they'd been looking for. Detectives now wanted to
determine whether more victims lay buried in the grounds
of the house.

Armin had confessed that he'd already digested as much as twenty kilograms of flesh from his slaughter victim's body, according to his own calculations. The police had confiscated about ten kilograms of human flesh from the freezer, which, if Armin was to be believed, meant he had stored about thirty kilograms of meat in total, an amount that indicated only one casualty. But the police needed to be certain no one else had been served up for dinner. As if expecting a reprieve for good behavior, Armin insisted he hadn't killed anybody else, but he admitted, "I would have done, though, if the opportunity had presented itself."

The dogs and the digger set to work on the rest of the garden, excavating the ground for nearly five hours. But the only other bodily remains they discovered looked distinctly canine. They belonged to Armin's old Alsation.

The arrival of the police earlier that morning had attracted attention in the normally subdued village. As the investigators continued their excavation work outside in the garden, in full view, the neighbors' curiosity mounted. Manfred Stück, Armin's childhood friend, came home as usual around midday for lunch. He drove past Armin's house and saw the police officers in Armin's garden, as well as a hearse outside. He hurried into his house to find out from his wife what had happened.

"Have you seen Armin's house?" he asked her. "The place is swarming with police. Have you any idea what's going on?"

Manfred's wife had indeed noticed all the action down the road at Armin's house, but she was as puzzled as he was to its cause. "I really hope that nothing dreadful has happened to him," Manfred said. "He may be a bit weird and all that, but he's not a bad sort really." The more Manfred reflected, though, the more he concluded something serious must have happened to poor old Armin. It was unusual for so many police to have turned up. And a hearse outside indicated that someone had died.

Armin's other neighbors were equally bewildered by the presence of the police. Nothing much ever happened in their idyllic little village; it was rare even to see a police car drive past, never mind have one purposefully stop at a resident's house and tear up the garden! The neighbors gossiped among themselves, but none of them dared go round to the house or telephone Armin.

Investigators continued to hunt inside Armin's house, as well as through the grounds. After five days, the police declared they had no evidence tying the self-confessed cannibal to other possible victims. Hans-Manfred Jung, prosecutor for the state of Hesse, concluded that Bernd had been Armin's only victim.

The news of Armin's atrocities spread through the neighborhood. Wicked and inhumane behavior had no place in a quiet town like Rotenburg. Evil like that belonged to the big city, or in sweat-drenched nightmares. Armin's neighbors simply couldn't comprehend what this man in their midst had done, and weren't keen to accept the reality of the news. They had been living next door to a monster! They had invited him into their houses to share coffee and cakes with them on Sunday afternoons. He had helped look after their children, for goodness' sake!

His neighbor Manfred was shocked. He had played with Armin as a child, had helped look after his pony; they had taken Armin's dog for walks through the local countryside together. They had served in the military together. Manfred had known Armin for *years*. Even though he would never have called him a friend, why hadn't he guessed that

Armin was a murderer? He'd always known Armin was strange, but he'd never imagined he was a killer.

Armin's former neighbor Nicole was equally astounded when she heard the news. "I heard it on the phone from a friend," Nicole told a neighbor. "She told me Armin had killed someone. My first thought was that he had been in a car crash and had killed someone accidentally. I just couldn't believe it. Armin was the kindest person under the sun."

Armin had shown a romantic interest in Nicole years earlier, while he was still hoping to find a woman to settle down with and build a family. Nicole used to ask him to come round and fix her computer. Armin would turn up at her house within a few minutes, ever eager to be of service. However, Nicole had dismissed any notion of anything other than friendship with him. "It would be like having a relationship with Mickey Mouse," she had said at the time.

Now Nicole had to wrestle with the concept that her kind and helpful Armin was actually a man-eater; ultimately she refused to acknowledge he was anything but the benevolent, compassionate man she had always taken him for. Armin was simply a misunderstood individual, with a problem, according to Nicole. He needed her help, and her friendship, she decided. She would stick by him, even if she couldn't comprehend why he had done such a terrible thing.

State psychiatrists, meanwhile, were also endeavoring to understand the motivations driving Armin's behavior. They weren't used to having a cannibal in their care, so they researched the subject, reading existing texts. They learned that a cannibal killer was usually introspective and withdrawn, with few associates and no close friends, and that he tended to enjoy solitary pursuits, such as watching horror movies. They were also aware that a cannibal killer often felt inadequate and inferior, except in regard to his crimes, which made his feel godlike.

Other characteristics included an elaborate fantasy life and a fascination with atrocities and cruelty; he often collected books or pictures of such images. A cannibal was usually under thirty-five, unmarried and of high intelligence. He tended to be sexually dysfunctional, with little or no experience of normal sexual intercourse. A cannibal killer often had a strong, ambivalent relationship with his mother, both loving and hating her. He was often seen as a "mama's boy" as an adult. He showed a great interest in pornography, particularly sadistic pornography. When captured and institutionalized in hospitals or prisons, a cannibal killer was usually very well behaved, which resulted in his being released or sent to a less secure unit.

Armin fitted their description perfectly.

Armin admitted to the state psychiatrists that he first dreamed of eating another man at an early age, and had harbored the desire for human flesh ever since. He often saw Bernd standing in front of him, he told the psychiatrists. In his imagination, he could still touch Bernd's body. And he felt more stable mentally since his friend had been inside him. He didn't feel as alone anymore; Bernd had filled his empty void.

Armin also told the psychiatrists that he had been able to absorb Bernd's masculinity, and had taken on some of Bernd's qualities and abilities. As an example, he claimed he could speak far better English than he could before he ate Bernd.

Asked why he had done it, Armin said, "I got a kick out of the idea of having another person inside of me." To Armin, his motivation was self-evident. "I had the fantasy and in the end I fulfilled it," he told the psychiatrists.

The state system didn't view Armin's cannibalism as simple goal fulfillment. They first examined the course of death and determined Bernd had been killed by a slit to the throat. The German authorities then filed murder charges against Armin. He was moved to a high-security prison, where he was to be kept for a year while he waited for his trial to begin.

Armin's lawyer, Harald Ermel, began putting together a case that would portray the cannibal in as wholesome a light as possible. Cannibalism was technically not a crime in Germany, he informed his client.

Armin was keen to point out that Bernd had *wanted* to be killed; that there was plenty of evidence in the form of numerous e-mail exchanges and the tape of slaughter that showed the consensual nature of Bernd's death.

Ermel proposed that his defendant should, at most, be convicted of "killing on demand." This charge was one generally confined to euthanasia cases. It carried a five-year term, maximum. Armin was eager to push for this charge.

He knew he faced a possible life sentence if found guilty of murder.

25

The
Cannibal
of Rotenburg

Katja Sandrock rubbed her eyes and yawned.

It was the morning of Wednesday, December 3, 2003, and Katja had left her parents' Rotenburg home not long after 2 A.M. The twenty-year-old was more used to falling *into* bed at such an early hour, not out of it. She rested her head on the shoulder of her eighteen-year-old friend, Jennifer Fey. The two had been waiting outside the courthouse since 4 A.M. in the hope of securing a ticket to see the latest media celebrity, Armin Meiwes, and attend his trial. Hanne Roland, eighteen, from the town of Ahnatal, and Fabienne Lorraine, seventeen, from Wolfhagen, had joined the girls shortly after 6 A.M. More competition, Katja thought and sighed.

Only the first thirty-six observers would get a place in the courtroom; members of the public who wanted to watch the trial had to stand in line each morning. Tickets for that day's proceedings were distributed at 8:30 A.M. The trial started at 9 A.M.

"I just can't believe he slaughtered that man like a pig," Fabienne said to Katja. She couldn't wait to tell her classmates about everything that would happen in court, and how scary the "Cannibal of Rotenburg" looked.

Katja knew Armin by sight, she boasted. In fact, she had seen him around Rotenburg lots of times.

The girls joined the gaggle of journalists and photographers assembled outside the court gates. The trial in Kassel's regional court was being billed as the country's first cannibalism prosecution case and had attracted so much attention, as one of the most extraordinary cases in German criminal history, that reporters had to participate in a lottery to get court seats as well. The Kassel court had been flooded with applications for the thirty-five available journalist seats and had awarded tickets to the media with the highest circulation and audience figures. The journalists' tickets guaranteed them seats for the entire trial, not just one day, like the spectators' tickets.

And then they saw him.

As one, a swarm of people flocked in Armin's direction. Elbows shoved, hands pushed and feet trampled. They were all desperate to see what the "Hannibal of Hesse" really looked like. Did he have red eyes, pointed teeth, a crazed expression? Would they immediately recognize him as a killer? Perhaps it wasn't safe to stand close to him; what if he attacked?

Used to the quiet of his solitary cell after a year in custody at Kassel-Wehlheiden prison, Armin was initially overwhelmed by the sea of bright lights that flashed in his direction, and the grasping crowd that greeted him. He granted the onlookers a slight smile as his eyes gradually adjusted to the glare. He had dressed carefully that morning, electing to wear his gray-blue suit, the one he kept for special occasions. He wore a charcoal-gray shirt underneath, which was set off by a discreetly patterned tie, and a pair of black shoes. On his left wrist was a leather wrist strap; on his right hand, a man's ring. His appearance was immaculate. Ermel, his lawyer, had brought his suits and other clothes to him in prison. Family members normally brought prisoners their clothes. Armin's family, however, didn't live nearby and were keen to distance themselves as much as possible from their cannibal relative.

Fabienne was disappointed.

The cannibal didn't look so scary after all. In fact, he appeared utterly respectable, dressed in his neat suit and tie. He wasn't what she'd expected; he looked so *ordinary,* the sort of man she saw every day and barely noticed. Armin walked past Fabienne and Katja into court, carrying a file under his arm. He adjusted his tie pin and checked that it was positioned correctly. He wanted to look his best in front of the panel of five judges. It was standard in German criminal cases involving a death to have a jury comprised of three professional judges as well as two members of the public, who were also referred to as judges, even though they didn't have any legal training. The trial would be led by the provincial presiding judge, Heinz-Völker Mütze. Dr. Alexander Wachter and Patrick Gerberding were the other legally trained judges. They would be joined on the panel by Rosamarie Lange and Günter Scholze. All five would make a decision on Armin's sentence.

The court and the observers arranged their various bags, cleared their throats and settled into their seats, as they prepared to listen to the charge brought against the self-confessed cannibal. The observers were separated from the rest of the courtroom by a one-meter-high barrier, which allowed them to watch everything taking place, but not to enter the room.

Marcus Köhler, the prosecuting attorney, watched Armin walk into court. It wasn't the first time he had seen Armin. Köhler had met him the morning after he confessed to the police.

The prosecuting attorney stood up and made the opening statement. He told the court that the forty-two-year-old subject, identified only as Armin M., stood accused of killing his victim, a computer chip developer at the Siemens corporation in Berlin, identified only as Bernd Juergen B., by stabbing him in the throat. Surnames aren't given out during German court cases, to protect individuals' privacy. The prosecutor told the court Armin had planned to sexually satisfy himself later with a videotape he had filmed of the act. Armin, he said, was charged with "murder for sexual satisfaction," a little-used murder statute Köhler was forced to employ as Germany had no laws against cannibalism. The prosecution also charged Armin with "disturbing the peace of the dead" for carving up Bernd's body.

Köhler told the court that between the date of Bernd's killing, March 9, 2001, and Armin's arrest in December 2002, the accused consumed most of Bernd's flesh, which he had stored in a freezer, in shrink-wrapped packages.

The accused spoke next. Armin stood up and faced the court as he prepared to give his statement. He had had plenty of time over the past twelve months to rehearse his words in his prison cell. He'd learned his speech almost by heart. And now he was ready to perform. The court was his stage and his audience was captive.

Armin endeavored to explain his motivations. He recalled the days of his childhood, when he had felt lonely and neglected after his father walked out on the family. He told the court he had fantasized about having a blond "younger brother," whom he could keep forever by "consuming him," and that he had first started thinking about cannibalism between the ages of eight and twelve, when he imagined eating schoolmates. Horror movies heightened his desires, he added. Armin revealed that "slim and blond" was the type of man he found appetizing, and admitted he found thoughts of cannibalism sexually arousing, but denied the charge of sexually motivated murder. "I didn't want to have sex with the partner I chose to slaughter. That had nothing to do with it," he stated to a stunned courtroom.

Armin ran through the events of March 9, 2001. He told the court how he had arranged via the Internet to meet his victim at Kassel train station, and that they discussed the impending slaughter in detail on arrival at his home in Rotenburg. Bernd had agreed to have sex with him, but afterward had second thoughts about going through with the rest, Armin said.

He then drove his guest back to the train station, where he bought a ticket to Berlin. But, changing his mind again, the victim decided to remain, and they returned to the house in Rotenburg.

Emotionless and calm, Armin recalled how he began the killing by cutting off Bernd's penis at his request, and told the court how they fried it in a pan and tried but failed to eat it.

Christine Reinckens, a talented court artist who drew detailed portraits and sketches of Armin, observed him carefully and grew accustomed to his athletic frame and the variety of expressions and stances that he employed. Her pencils and crayons carefully translated his face, body and moods into images on paper.

Christine watched Armin stand stiffly in front of the court, holding his hands either crossed or folded in front of him. She listened to Armin prefix nearly every sentence or reply with a "Yes, well." And she noted how well presented Armin was in his tailored suit. She noticed that he normally wore glasses, but took them off whenever photographs were being taken. It was obvious to her that the accused man was vain.

Christine found the cold, dispassionate manner in which Armin described his crimes almost as horrifying as the acts themselves. He didn't flinch when giving detailed descriptions of how he had chopped up and consumed his victim's body. You would have thought that he was in court for losing his driving license or some other minor offense, from the matter-of-fact way in which he spoke, Christine reflected.

Armin told the courtroom how the victim moved to the bathroom and lay in the bath as he bled to death. His penis was cut off at 8:30 P.M. and then at 4 A.M. he was stabbed in the throat and died.

"I kissed him once more, prayed and pleaded for forgiveness," Armin announced to a sea of horrified faces. "My friend enjoyed dying, death," Armin reasoned with them. "I only waited horrified for the end after doing the deed," namely the stabbing. "It took so terribly long."

Armin admitted that after killing Bernd he subsequently looked for further willing victims through Internet ads and chat rooms. He showed neither guilt nor regret to the crowd in court. Killing and eating Bernd had been the biggest kick of his life and he derived pleasure from remembering it. "Show me the statute where it states that what I've done is against the law!" he said with a smile to the prosecution.

He had used his time in prison to gain a good grasp of the law and was well aware that the charge against him stood on shaky ground. He had also enjoyed talking about his experiences with the prison psychiatrists over the past year, and incorporated terms learned from the sessions into his everyday vocabulary. He had "internalized his brother," he told the court.

Armin was pleased with his performance on the first day of the trial.

He had spoken for hours, declaring what he thought was right and wrong, always holding a book in his hand. His attorney, in contrast, hardly said a word. This was Armin's show, and he was loath to cede the floor.

26

No Signs of Psychiatric Illness

The first day of Armin's trial was reported around the world. Newspapers, radio and television programs discussed the brutality of the night of horror, a crime beyond most people's comprehension. It was evil not seen in Germany since the depravities of the Nazis, and around the globe people waited at the edge of their seats. Would the criminal lawyers be able to defend human dignity against this ugly boil that had erupted through the crust of social convention?

Armin came across as a serious bank clerk, the type of respectable man every mother wants her daughter to bring home. He simply wasn't the lurid type of maniac people expected; he was a suburban cannibal. His very ordinariness, the shocking discrepancy between the person Armin *seemed* to be and what he had *done,* disturbed people greatly.

• • •

The witnesses started giving testimony on the second day of the trial.

The first witness sat alone on the witness stand, surrounded on four sides, by the defense, the panel of judges, the prosecution and the expert witnesses. He had a small build and black, spiky hair. His smart suit hung on hollow shoulders. He was called Dirk and was one of the men who had visited Armin but failed to stay for dinner. Dirk had backed out of being slaughtered after Armin had shown him a photograph of one of his previous guests, taken as the man was hanging upside down from a meat hook in the abattoir.

The German national was an event manager and conference organizer who had worked for hotels in London before subsequently losing his job amid the media attention surrounding the cannibal scandal.

The next witness, Jakob, appeared in court disguised in a black scarf wrapped tightly around his face, with just his eyes showing. He had to adjust it to hear the judge speak. A former neighbor of Armin's, he was a good-looking man, with tight, black curls. He was in his mid-twenties and lived off the state, the court learned. At the age of sixteen, Jakob had started playing homosexual games with Armin, who was in his mid-thirties at the time. The games lasted a few years, he recalled. The two had been friends and had watched homosexual pornographic films together before having sex. Jakob started most of his replies with the phrase "It's normal anyhow." He stressed that cannibalism was never involved in these games. That clearly *wasn't* normal to Jakob.

Another of the men who had acted out slaughter role-plays with Armin was brought into the witness stand. Jörg, thirty-four from Villingen, in southern Germany, wore skiing goggles and a baseball cap with earflaps to avoid being recognized. He told the court of his close escape. He testified that he removed his clothes shortly after arriving at the farmhouse, that Armin smeared his body in oil, marked it for butchering and strung him up on a pulley. Feeling ill, Jörg had asked Armin to let him off the hook, literally. Jörg left Armin's house soon afterward, he told the court.

Stefan, another witness who had played slaughter games, wore a baseball hat, sunglasses and a smart coat as his disguise. This witness worked locally as a teacher in Kassel and was keen not to be recognized. He narrated his association with Armin, telling the court how they had exchanged slaughter fantasies.

Another witness, Daniel, also wore a disguise in court. He wrapped himself in a black scarf and wore a brown bomber jacket and a woolly hat to hide from the spectators' prying eyes. Daniel testified that he had offered himself to Armin for dinner but had been turned down because he was "too fat."

Next to appear in court was Martina, the nearest thing to a girlfriend and a proper relationship Armin ever had. Martina made a bizarre impression, appearing in a strawberry-colored wig the kind of thick black glasses you would normally buy in a joke shop. She sat clutching her black handbag in her lap, with her hands crossed in front of her in a protective pose. The divorcée said she and her three children had moved away from Rotenburg during her thirties, and she maintained that nothing had ever happened between her and Armin, that they had just flirted. The couple had fallen apart when Martina informed Armin that she was going to be sterilized; he wanted a "fertile" woman that could bear him children.

Armin contradicted her story and said that he and Martina had gone to bed together; the court let it pass and moved their attention to the next witness, Marion. She was a former neighbor and had set Armin up with Martina. Marion was well-off and had moved from Wüstefeld to a large house in nearby Rotenburg. She and Armin used to walk their dogs together, she told the spectators. Armin was a good man, who was sensitive and friendly, she told the court. "He came across as being very childlike," she said. Marion had regularly visited Armin during the year he was in prison, and she wrote him letters. Their relationship was purely platonic, she stressed—there was no romance.

The next witness was Armin's half-brother, Ingbert. It was his wife Armin had spoken to before confessing his crime to his lawyer. The forty-eight year old wore glasses and had black hair, which he brushed back from his forehead. He had the same chin, lips and facial expressions as Armin. Ingbert didn't speak in court. He chose to have his statement read out instead. "Armin enjoyed making model houses and playing in the garden." Ingbert claimed he had never noticed Armin displaying any particular interest in violence or the slaughter of animals. Nor had Armin ever spoken about cannibalism to him. "He was a completely normal boy; he had fights occasionally with other children," according to Ingbert. He was amazed, he told the court, when he learned about what Armin had done.

Armin's other half-brother, Wolfgang the priest, didn't attend the trial. Wolfgang hadn't visited Armin while he was in prison and he refused to testify on his behalf. Armin's father also chose not to speak in court, or give a statement.

Witnesses associated with Bernd were also given a turn to speak in court.

Bernd's father, a prominent Berlin doctor, didn't testify. He was too shocked. Rene, Bernd's boyfriend, told the court his lover had expressed "no thoughts of suicide." He said Bernd hadn't shown any indication that he was planning to die, and that they had been planning a holiday together. Rene still couldn't believe what had happened. It simply didn't make sense, he told the court. Bernd's ex-girlfriend, Petra, also appeared as a witness. She wore a bomber jacket, had short hair, walked like a man and gave an overall masculine impression. What's more, Petra and Rene looked quite similar. She told the court Bernd had never had suicidal tendencies. Daniela, another ex-girlfriend, told the court of Bernd's conversion from heterosexual to homosexual, and of his desire for more hardcore, unusual sex as their relationship progressed.

The court also learned how Bernd had grown more demanding when having sex with prostitutes. Immanuel, one of Bernd's regulars, told the court that "mostly Bernd wasn't happy; he was addicted to sex." The good-looking, exotic man talked about how Bernd had repeatedly urged him to bite and then amputate his penis, and how Immanuel had dismissed these requests as mere erotic games. "Once, I brought a knife to him during sex, and told him I was going to cut it off, but I thought it was fantasy," he said, pausing to cry before finishing. "Unfortunately, he really had it done."

Immanuel's revelation led to more than an hour of discussion between the prosecution and the defense about the exact meaning of Bernd's request, as they tried to establish whether Bernd had asked to be eaten by others before making Armin's acquaintance.

Victor, a former prostitute, also spoke to the court of Bernd's pathologic desire to have his penis bitten off. "When he offered me ten thousand marks to do it, I finally broke off contact with him," the thirty-eight-year-old man stated.

But Bernd soon found another man who was prepared to carry out his bizarre fantasy; this the court already knew.

The court was shown some visual evidence to illustrate Armin's crime.

The presiding judge, Mütze, brought out exhibits from another room, unpacked them and laid them out for all to see. The court took a collective intake of breath as they looked at Armin's weapons of death, namely six knives, an axe and a meat grinder.

The slaughter tools weren't half as gruesome, however, as the next exhibit—the three videocassettes used to record the slaughter.

The media and observers were ushered outside; only Armin, the two attorneys, the five members of the jury, the expert witnesses and the court reporter were allowed to watch the video. Scholze, a member of the public who was serving on the jury, later admitted he pretended he was watching an educational documentary while he witnessed Armin use a saw to portion out human flesh like a butcher. Fellow jury member Rosamarie Lange almost fainted as Armin talked to Bernd's severed head while he disembow-eled the body, hung from a butcher's hook in his slaughter room.

Police who had seen the tape of the entire ordeal admit-ted they had undergone psychological counseling. "I'd never seen anything like it in my career," declared federal investigator Wilfried Fehl. "It's a thing that's practically unimaginable even for experienced criminologists. I had to vomit. It leads us to where thinking stops."

The viewers were relieved as the video stopped, just af-ter Bernd's death. If eating Bernd's flesh was what gave Armin the big kick, then why didn't he just film the eat-ing? the prosecutor asked the courtroom. Why film the slaughter?

The court learned (to their disbelief) from investigator Fehl that the gruesome case before them was not an iso-lated one. His officers had discovered a flourishing canni-bal scene in Germany. "We are talking about dentists, teachers, cooks, government officials and handymen," Fehl told the court. Rudolf Egg, a criminologist in the German central criminal service, informed the court that there were *several hundred* people with cannibalistic tendencies in Germany alone, and many thousands around the world. But the criminologist was keen to point out that, unlike Armin, only a tiny proportion of those entering cannibal chat rooms were willing to follow through and meet in real life.

Police investigator Wolfgang Buch spoke of the secret online lives that had brought Armin and Bernd together. Both had become chat-room addicts, hanging out in rooms such as the Cannibal Cafe. Armin's e-mail correspondence with other members of cannibal forums would fill two trucks if it were printed out, Inspector Isolde Stock added.

Judge Mütze spent hours reading Armin and Bernd's e-mail correspondence to the court. He repeated the swear words and sexual descriptions that littered their e-mail exchanges in the same monotone in which he read the more mundane passages. The judge also read out Armin's fantasy story about the prostitute that had been published on the Internet. Armin smiled proudly as he listened to the story's description of the big, hot jets of blood pulsating out of the prostitute's chest as he was stabbed.

Expert witnesses were brought forth to determine whether the self-confessed cannibal was criminally liable.

A prison psychiatrist, Heinrich Wilmer, testified that the accused was in good mental health but should be given psychotherapy. He said the defendant had a "personality disorder, lacking empathy and self-control."

Klaus Beier, a psychotherapist and sexologist based at Berlin's Charite hospital, concurred that Armin couldn't be classified as mentally ill, and shouldn't be sent to a mental hospital. Beier said Armin had "at least average intelligence and showed no signs of psychiatric illness." Armin, a loner, had developed his fascination with cannibalism as a way of "being close" to men. Early in his life, Armin had apparently fantasized about having a friend who would never leave him, Beier said. The arrival of the Internet and e-mail had encouraged him to act out that fantasy. Armin's act was a wholly selfish one, Beier told the court. "With this act, Meiwes thought only of his goal, not of Brandes's needs."

Armin allowed very few cracks to appear in his poise during the trial, but when Beier asked him the difference between sex and eroticism, his mask slipped for an instant and the courtroom caught a glimpse of his inner chaos.

"Sex is hardcore in bed," Armin replied to Beier's question and then fell silent, a flush of red embarrassment spreading across his face. "Erotic is something which is nice to look at."

Another expert witness, psychiatrist and psychology professor Georg Stolpmann, was called. He described Armin as "extremely smug and self-assured" and as having a "schizoid personality" but said he detected no indication of mental illness. "He carried out an act that was planned and prepared," Stolpmann said. He felt Armin had been subconsciously trying to consume a human being to fill the void caused by the departure of his father and his brothers, which left him to care for his domineering mother until her death. He explained to the court that Armin had assumed many of his mother's characteristics after her death, adding her personality traits to his own. He had become authoritarian, for example.

Stolpmann and Beier both mentioned Armin's alleged abuse by an older relative, which he talked to them about in sessions prior to the trial. Armin told them that when he was a child, he spent hours watching gay porno videos with this relative. According to Armin, this relative encouraged him to act out the scenes. The two expert witnesses indicated that Armin may not have deliberately lied about the abuse, but it may have been something he invented and chose to believe.

Ermel was pleased with the expert witnesses' conclusions regarding his client's sanity. According to their testimony, Armin could *not* be classified as mentally ill and was criminally liable. He had feared that if his forty-two year old client were sent to a psychiatric institution, he could be kept there for many years and possibly for the rest of his life.

Armin smiled too as heard himself pronounced sane. He knew he was of sound mind. How ridiculous that he would be considered mentally instable, when cannibalism was the most natural thing in the world to him.

27

A Complicated
Matter

It was the twelfth day of the trial. The witnesses and expert witnesses had spent ten days testifying. Now it was the attorneys' turn to address the jury.

The prosecuting attorney, Köhler, stood up and made his statement. He acknowledged to the court that the victim was willing to die. Bernd had repeatedly said that on the videotape of his slaughter. He added, however, that the victim *may* have been incapable of rational thought, and that the accused took advantage of Bernd's state of mind. Köhler pushed for a life sentence, on the basis that Armin was simply too dangerous to ever be released. Murder carries a minimum fifteen-year-to-life sentence in Germany.

Armin's attorney, Ermel, wearing a purple suit, listened carefully to the prosecutor's case and exchanged an occasional joke with his client. He pressed for the lesser "killing on demand" charge. It carried a maximum five-year jail sentence and was normally applied in cases of "mercy killing." Ermel knew the question of consent was crucial; he contended that Bernd had wanted to be killed and was aware of his fate. He stressed to the court how Bernd's e-mails had clearly spelled out his willingness to die. He told the court one of the e-mails read: "There's absolutely no way back for me, only forwards, through your teeth."

The defendant and his attorney stood side by side, their shoulders nearly always touching as they mirrored each other's body language. Ermel's support for Armin was apparent for all in the court to see.

"My client is not a monster," Ermel declared. He presented Armin instead as "psychologically disturbed," and claimed "he has a sexual makeup that is fixated on human flesh." He also described Armin as a "gentleman of the old school." Armin's female witnesses, namely Martina and Marion, his former neighbor, had commented on Armin's manners and politeness, the lawyer said.

On the thirteenth day of the trial, Armin was due to speak.

He reflected on the events so far, and on all the evidence that had been given. Overall he felt the trial had gone well. He had enjoyed revealing his fantasies to the crowds of spectators, and reliving the details of his act of cannibalism. So many people had assembled on his behalf, all of them wanting to discuss him and his beloved slaughter, that he felt important and flattered. It was wonderful attracting so much attention and being the object of media frenzy. He stood firmly in center stage nowadays and he loved it.

The trial had given him the chance to bring his memories to life in front of a global audience, and it was such a relief not to have to conceal his moment of glory anymore. It frustrated him that people didn't really understand how wonderful it had all felt, but he couldn't help that; they lived in a world of different values. He believed he had done his best to explain, and he hoped at least some of them now understood the reasons behind his actions.

He also hoped he had convinced some people in court of his innocence.

Bernd had *wanted* to die; Armin had merely *assisted* him.

He had admittedly used Bernd to fulfill his own fantasies, but it had been with his prior knowledge and consent. Armin realized he needed to make a powerful closing statement to persuade the people in court to see Bernd's death from his point of view and not that of the prosecution's.

He stood up, crossed his hands in front of himself and faced the court. He was aware of how important these last words were; his closing statement could decide his future. He needed to engage the courtroom's sympathy, to get them to like him, and not view him as a monster.

"My friend enjoyed dying, death," he said. "For him, it was a nice death."

The spectators shuddered, Rene looked dismayed, and Bernd's friends appeared upset. Armin's crime didn't cease to shock, even after thirteen days of hearing about it in court: being stabbed in the throat, having your body cut into pieces and digested was a pleasant way to leave this world?

"Bernd came to me of his own free will to end his life," Armin declared.

He stressed that Bernd had freely accepted the fate that awaited him, that both of them had been involved in the planning of their contract of self-destruction and flesh. Each had agreed to the other's terms, including the term of death, he stressed. He was keen to make the court understand that he wasn't a brutal monster who had ripped out his victim's heart and lungs against his will, or crept up on him before stabbing him to death by surprise; he didn't want to be classified as a cold-blooded murderer. He had only killed someone who had consented to it. He had *freed* the other men who hadn't consented to be turned into his next dinner, he reminded the court.

Well aware that eating another human being wasn't tolerated behavior in society, even if it was the most natural thing in the world to him, he replied, "I accept this is taboo," in response to a question from the prosecution, who could interrupt a closing statement. The question was whether or not the concept of "taboo" meant anything to him.

Nonetheless, Armin insisted he could vindicate his crime.

"I know I have to justify what I did to God and the world," he said. He shrugged his shoulders as he said it, as if to indicate he couldn't even start to come to terms with other people's morals. Armin didn't cry, weep or seem at all sad that Bernd had died. Nor did he seem to feel any remorse. His biggest regret, he told the court, was that he hadn't gotten to know his victim better before stabbing him to death. Yet he insisted that he lamented the killing. "I regret much, but I can't undo it," he said. He also insisted he had satisfied his hunger for human flesh. "I had my big kick and I don't need to do it again," he claimed. "I didn't want to kill or hurt anybody," he added.

Armin sat down after he had finished making his statement. He had done his best, and soon he would return to the solitary confinement of his prison cell. He didn't think he would stay there long, however. "I think I will be out after four or maybe five years," he said. "It isn't as if I killed anybody against their will."

Observers of the trial were not as convinced Armin would be let off with a mild sentence; however, the case was the first of its kind, and cannibalism wasn't illegal in Germany, which made everything more difficult to predict. It was difficult even for legal experts to define the crime. Professor Arthur Kreuzer of the Institute for Criminology at Giessen University, Germany, believed the complexity of the trial would lead to the proceedings becoming a benchmark case.

"It is unique that we are leveling the severest charge of murder against someone and yet have to admit that the victim, whether disturbed or not, wanted it," Kreuzer said. "The killer sought out his victim and the victim sought out his killer." In Kreuzer's view, the court wasn't dealing with a murder case. "This is killing undertaken for both the killer and victim and can't be regarded as the worst case of premeditated killing." Yet Kreuzer also disagreed with the defense's proposed charge of mercy killing. "I don't think it is killing on request either, because it was not an altruistic, but an egoistic deed," he stated. Kreuzer expected the case to go as high as Germany's Federal Constitutional Court. And he expected prosecutors to have to consult new medical experts to assess Armin's mental state, despite the fact that the initial tests showed it to be intact.

Observers of the trial around the globe debated what sentence the modern-day cannibal should be charged with; their opinions, however, wouldn't influence the length of Armin's prison sentence. That responsibility, and the formal definition of his crime, ultimately lay with the five-judge jury that had listened to him give evidence in Kassel regional court. Heinz-Völker Mütze, the provincial presiding judge, was the man who, assisted by his jury, had to decide whether Armin Meiwes had murdered or killed someone. It was a difficult decision to make, even for an experienced judge like him. He knew he needed more time before announcing his decision.

"In many cases, the court would announce its verdict on the last day of proceedings," Mütze said. "But this is such a complicated matter. I hope to have a ruling by January 30."

Armin's future was to remain undecided for a little while longer.

28

Manslaughter

It was Friday, January 30, and a cold winter's day. The chill of the morning air seemed to creep under the clothes and sink into the bones of the people who were huddled together outside Kassel regional court. They rubbed their hands together, stamped their feet and nursed flasks of hot tea in a bid to get warm.

The crowd had gathered outside the doors of the court by 5:15 A.M., determined to fight for the limited number of tickets available to see Armin Meiwes. Today he was due to be sentenced in court, and they were prepared to wait up to four hours in the bitter cold for the privilege of witnessing the event firsthand. Tickets would be awarded only to the first thirty-six people, at 8:30 A.M., before the trial started at 9 A.M.; those who failed to get a ticket would have to make do with a quick glimpse of Armin as he entered the court.

When the self-confessed cannibal, whose trial had riveted Germany and the rest of the world arrived, he appeared outwardly calm and composed. He looked as immaculate as ever in a dark suit and a gray-and-yellow tie.

Journalists and cameramen jostled for position to get near enough to ask a pertinent question or take a telling photograph of Germany's notorious cannibal.

Yes, he felt good, Armin told the questioning reporters, folding his hands in front of him and smiling. "I slept well." He grinned for the cameras before he was allowed inside the courtroom for the final session to begin.

The suspense in the courtroom was palpable.

Eyes stared at Judge Mütze from all corners of the room, trying to read his expression as they waited for the verdict to be announced. How would this unspeakable crime fit into Germany's modern legal system? Most observers of the trial were convinced Armin Meiwes, accused of killing a computer specialist from Berlin, eating his genitalia and then freezing the rest of his body for later repasts, would be convicted of murder.

They were wrong.

Armin Meiwes was convicted of manslaughter.

He was sentenced to eight years and six months in prison, and allowed time off for good behavior, meaning that he could walk free in as little as four years and three months. There were several seconds of stunned silence after the verdict was announced, then the room erupted into loud whispers. Courtroom spectators shook their heads in disbelief; Bernd's friends and Rene, his former partner, looked appalled.

Judge Mütze watched the room full of surprised faces and listened to the murmur of voices. He addressed the spectators and said Armin had committed "a behavior which is condemned in our society, namely the killing and butchering of a human being." He further stated that

Armin's deed was "viewed with revulsion." However, he continued, the very clear video evidence showed him *not* to be guilty of murder. "Seen legally, this is manslaughter, killing a person without being a murderer," he explained. "The famous lust for murder was not there," Mütze added. "There were no base motives."

In the judge's opinion, the crime would have been more serious if Bernd had been killed for money rather than for nourishment. The desire to eat the flesh of a fellow citizen did not constitute a base motive!

The judge pointed out that Armin found killing Bernd to be "very unpleasant." Some thought this made Armin *more* culpable, since he had to overcome a natural revulsion to the act of killing, unlike many impulsive or psychopathic murderers who have no qualms about the act at all. Yet that was not the judge's opinion. He said that, further, Armin had a terrible psychological predicament. Judge Mütze described to the courtroom how the accused had been plagued by cannibalistic feelings since he was a boy and had long fantasized about eating people. The stab in Bernd's throat, the judge said, had been a "necessary evil" to "fulfill his slaughter fantasies." According to the judge's implicit argument, Armin couldn't help having cannibal desires, any more than he could help being the height he was or the color of his hair—therefore it would be wrong, morally, to punish him for those desires. The consumption of Bernd's flesh didn't constitute "a classic case of cannibalism" in the judge's opinion. The primary motive had been "the wish to make another man part of himself," and Armin had reached this "bonding experience" through the consumption of human flesh.

The judge recognized that the trial had made the public familiar with the dark world of sado-eroticism and cannibalism. "We've seen people growing accustomed to a subculture that we couldn't have imagined existed before the trial," he said. "We've opened a door that we would rather close again but which shows how many people in need of help live out their fantasies on the Internet." Mütze acknowledged the role that the World Wide Web had played in the crime. "The Internet made the act possible," he said. "Two mentally disturbed people met each other there and reached an agreement. It was ethically and morally despicable, but both of them didn't care about that." He said of the two men, "They were two deeply psychologically disturbed people who both wanted something from the other."

There was a slight grimace on Armin's face as the verdict was read out in court. He was looking thinner and paler than when the trial had started. He sat quietly, though, as the judge gave his explanations.

Armin's lawyer was pleased with the sentence. Ermel considered it a "partial success" as the sentence came out nearer his wishes than the prosecution's demand of fifteen years for murder. He said, "At the trial, Meiwes opened his soul to the world and everyone knew what he was saying was the absolute truth." In further defense of his client, he said, "He would never have eaten his victim against his wishes, and when he has served his time he will have plenty to look forward to."

But others in the spectator room—the judge's explanations notwithstanding—were very disturbed by the verdict. They agreed Armin should not be punished for *having* his fantasies, but felt he *should* be punished for *acting* upon them. They reasoned that Armin Meiwes wasn't the only person to suffer from unacceptable fantasies—yet others managed to suppress their urges and go about their daily business without harming others. Furthermore, hadn't the judge himself pointed out that Armin's act of cannibalism was the outcome of a lifelong psychological quirk? The court-appointed psychiatrist had said this "quirk" was not changeable by medical or any other means. In other words, was there any reason to suppose Armin would stop having cannibal fantasies? It seemed unlikely; he had continued to advertise for victims after he had eaten and disposed of Bernd. Therefore, wasn't there every reason to suspect he would continue to be a very dangerous man?

Armin got up and made his way out of the courtroom. He knew the verdict was a good result; he'd been spared a murder conviction.

He was already seen as a model prisoner in custody—if he kept up the good behavior, he could look forward to drinking his favorite South African red again at a sidewalk cafe in a few years. He recognized someone he knew in the observer room on his way out, nodded to him in a friendly manner and smiled. Then he went down the stairs and into the green police van that was waiting to take him back to his home for the next few years, his solitary cell in Kassel-Wehlheiden prison.

Outside Kassel regional court the spectators discussed the relatively light sentence the judge had handed down. Armin could be out on parole, and trawling the Internet for fresh victims, in four years and three months, they whispered to each other.

"Terrible, terrible, it can't be true," said an elderly woman, who had stormed out of the courtroom. Allan Hall, who had traveled from London to see the trial, was "puzzled" by the mildness of the sentence. "I just can't understand it," he said. "Eight-and-half years for a crime like that? It was murder at the end of the day." Manfred Schübel from Kassel, who had followed the court case, agreed. "The sentence is far too mild," he said. He may not have behaved like a cannibal during the trial but "in my mind he's still dangerous." Edgar Posner from Kassel, who had also watched the trial, agreed that the sentence was too lax.

"In my opinion, he should be locked away." Bernd Exner told reporters, "It's too lenient; he should have got life. Society needs to be protected from people like that." Deaconess Gisela Strohriegl considered what Armin had done to be "unbelievably and inconceivably horrible." She hoped his alleged faith and the fact that he went to church would teach him to see his crime in a different light and "take responsibility for it before God."

A minority of people who watched the trial, such as Werner Diegler, thought manslaughter was the right sentence. The victim had given his consent to be killed, they pointed out.

In general, however, even the most liberal of Germans were taken aback by the lightness of the sentence and the implicit suggestion that eating one's fellow human beings for pleasure was just another lifestyle choice. Outraged citizens wondered why, if international police were going to hunt down pedophile Web sites and the men who visited them, a similar approach could not be taken with chat rooms in which men arranged to have themselves slaughtered like animals for a turn-on! What took place in the bedrooms—or dining rooms—of the nation was people's own business, but surely it couldn't be legal to eat people! *Even if* they requested to be on the menu! In a civilized country like Germany limits had to be set and guidelines established.

Former colleagues and friends of Bernd or Armin were relieved that the trial had finally reached a conclusion, even if they didn't agree with the sentence.

Stefan Pommerening, who had worked with Bernd at Siemens and had followed the trial in the newspapers, still couldn't believe that his former colleague had wanted to be eaten. "It was a completely different Bernd from the one we knew. It never would have crossed our minds. We never would have imagined it." Angela Hobeck, another of Bernd's former colleagues, also declared she "couldn't believe it."

"I got an e-mail one morning saying Bernd had been found," Hobeck said. "There was an attachment with a newspaper link. They used the same photo of Bernd they had used when they were searching for him. It must have been a second personality that he had inside him. He must have been very good at pretending."

Armin's former colleagues were also horrified when they learned of his crimes. They recalled with a shudder the meatballs and savory snacks he had brought to the office and felt relieved that he had never offered them around.

However, it was the people of Rotenburg who were probably most scarred by Armin's cannibalism. Their idealized rural life had been destroyed by his flesh-eating, and now that the sensational trial was over, they simply wanted to shut their doors on the media frenzy and try to restore the peaceful existence they had previously enjoyed.

The whole case was incomprehensible for Armin's immediate neighbors, who hadn't suspected any of it. Manfred Stück, Armin's neighbor and childhood friend, worried that Armin would kill again, given the opportunity; he believed the only reason he hadn't killed a second time was he hadn't succeeded in locating a suitable victim before he was arrested. Neighbor Karl-Friedrich Schnaar didn't expect Armin to lose his urge to eat human flesh by being locked behind prison bars. "He's not getting any help in there," he said. "His world in prison will be suspended in time. He's going to be reliving all of this during the time that he serves inside. It's not going to let him move on. He's going to be a ticking time bomb when he comes out."

The residents of Rotenburg didn't want Armin back once he had served his sentence. "The shock has been massive," said Schnaar. "I don't think anybody has thought about how they could help Armin, or if he needs a jacket, or cigarettes brought to him [in prison]. That hasn't been the case at all. And there's still the burning question, why? We won't get an answer to that for sure." Schnaar suspected Armin was enjoying his newfound fame. "He had a real inferiority complex and now he has power, now he's really someone."

Other associates of Armin felt they had been deceived and doubted their friendship could be salvaged. "I don't think I would go sailing with him again," said Heribert Brinkmann, the skipper from Armin's sailing holiday. "The trust has gone. Not just a little bit, but completely. I don't know if I could get other people to go. Well, maybe we might go just one more time to see what happens. The crew is stronger than him and we could keep an eye on him. If the worse came to the worst, we could always throw him overboard. It would be the easiest way to get rid of him."

29

Appeals

Armin felt comfortable within the confines of his cell. He wore the standard uniform of Kassel prison inhabitants—dark blue trousers and a sky-blue shirt over a white T-shirt—neatly pressed, with the shirt tidily tucked into his trousers.

He had grown up in a disciplinarian environment, and was used to receiving orders from his mother and army officers, so he found a certain reassurance in the prison's daily routine. In prison, there were clear guidelines as to what was right and what was wrong, and what was expected of you. It was a relief to be given orders to follow. There wasn't any stress or responsibility or expectations in prison, just routine. His days blended into one another.

Armin also liked the male environment. Everywhere he turned there were men. He could indulge himself by watching some of the fit, young inmates when he took a shower, and could breathe in the smell of their sweat and body odors. Testosterone dominated the atmosphere along the prison corridors.

Most of all, though, Armin enjoyed the status his crime had brought him. Eating Bernd had given him notoriety, and his reputation as "The Cannibal" had spread throughout the prison, courtesy of newspapers and rumors, even before his arrival. Gone were the days when Armin Meiwes was a nobody; nowadays everyone seemed to have heard of him and his crime.

What's more, fellow inmates soon recognized Armin's intelligence, and respected and admired him for it. Armin had spent hours studying the German legal system before and after his trial, and the prisoners sought legal advice from him; he also penned eloquent letters for other inmates, thinking of clever ways to express what they wanted to say. This popularity didn't mean that he wasn't feared— he was. Armin's cannibalistic ways weren't something other criminals could readily identify with, and that made him frightening. The prisoners knew it wasn't wise to mess around with someone who would eat you for supper.

Armin also kept himself busy answering an ever-growing pile of personal mail. He tapped away on the old prison typewriter, replying to fan mail from his many admiring correspondents. He was additionally inundated with requests for interviews, which he declined—unless the publication was prepared to pay him well. He had begun thinking about his career, and how he could secure his future fame and fortune. He believed a host of exciting career opportunities were open to him, and that he had his prison term (if he served his full manslaughter sentence) to fully focus on making the most of them.

His first proposed project was an autobiography. He loved telling the details of Bernd's slaughter, and he was keen to relive the experience by putting pen to paper. His lawyer informed him that publishers were already fighting for the rights to this proposed book. He just needed to pick a publisher that would him pay handsomely. Armin told his lawyer that by writing his life story, he could deter anyone with similar fantasies who wanted to copy him. "They should go for treatment," Armin said of any would-be cannibals, "so it doesn't escalate like it did with me."

His other key project was a film about his life. His lawyer had told him the film rights to his life story could net more than $1 million. Admittedly, Armin would have to pay back the cost of the trial, estimated at about $140,000, but he still could be rich when he returned home, if a movie came to fruition. Armin estimated he could end up earning more money for being a real cannibal than actor Anthony Hopkins earned for playing the fictitious man-eater Hannibal Lecter in the film *The Silence of the Lambs*. And according to his lawyer, a bidding war had broken out for the rights to this autobiographical film. When his lawyer was asked who was bidding, Ermel replied, "At this point, I'm contractually bound not to give out the name of the company." He also said, "But it's early days and we're getting more offers all the time."

All the attention surrounding Armin in his new environment started to make him feel like a VIP. He normally behaved like a model prisoner, ever conscious that he could be released on parole for good behavior in half that time *if* he were good. But occasionally, his exaggerated self-importance spilled over into his dealings with the prison officials.

Christmas was one such occasion.

Armin requested that he be served a giant sausage for his Christmas dinner, and sickened prison authorities by asking for the eight-inch Bockwurst banger to be cooked in garlic and white wine—the same recipe he had used to braise Bernd's body parts.

"It's obviously his idea of a sick joke," a prison official said. "He can have the sausage, but it won't be done his way."

The animal rights group PETA (People for the Ethical Treatment of Animals) were interested in Armin's menu on Christmas Day. They sent him a vegetarian cookbook and a Christmas hamper full of veggie burgers and Tofu products. PETA hoped the vegetarian starter kit would persuade Armin to mend his ways and join their vegetarian ranks. "What this man did to a German computer expert is done to other creatures every day," explained PETA spokesman Juergen Faulmann. "The cruel scenario of slaughtering, cutting up, portioning, freezing and eating of body parts is the grim reality for more than 450 million sentient individuals that are killed in this country every year," he said.

Armin failed to be convinced by PETA's argument in favor of vegetarianism.

In the world outside prison walls, Armin's fame continued to grow.

His widely publicized act of cannibalism made him a big star in the cannibal scene—he was renowned for actually having killed and eaten someone, not just talking about it. Disturbingly, a number of Web sites dedicated to Armin appeared, with people advertising for willing victims. Armin's story had proved to them that it *was* possible to go out and eat a fellow human being—and be let off with a light sentence.

Few of Armin's former acquaintances came to visit him in prison. His only regular visitor was Marion Reich, who continued to view him in a benevolent light. "He is and remains a person. He was always nice and kind. Also to my children," Marion said of Armin. She insisted the relationship was purely platonic, denying media reports to the contrary. "Just because I haven't turned my back on him, then I'm suddenly a cannibal's darling. It's bad enough that his family has turned away from from him. I'm not alone. My father and my friend Meike Stück are sticking by him. Even my sister has been to see him in prison." Armin's former neighbor said she could imagine him finding a place in society again, although she admitted it would be "difficult." "Murderers who murder people maliciously or violate children also find a place in society. And I find them a lot worse than Mr. Meiwes. Mr. Meiwes isn't dangerous for the general public. He has learned how to function."

Marion and Armin kept in touch by letter too. In one, he said he was a "heap of sorrow, when I'm alone," in his cell. And he was ashamed, Armin wrote. His words toughened Marion's resolve. She was determined to be there for him when he needed her.

Armin hoped his lawyer could win a shorter sentence for him via an appeal. He wanted Ermel to push for one based on a charge of "killing on demand" rather than manslaughter. "Killing on demand" could carry a minimum sentence of only six months, extending up to five years.

German prosecutors were also eager to appeal; they wanted the manslaughter conviction overturned too.

Labeling Armin a "human butcher" who acted to "satisfy a sexual impulse," they said Armin should have known his victim was disturbed and not taken advantage of his state of mind. Prosecutor Köhler planned to charge Armin on two counts during an appeal, firstly for killing the victim and secondly for eating human flesh. Armin was guilty of "murder for sexual satisfaction" and of "disturbing the peace of the dead," the prosecutor maintained. If Armin were sentenced for murder, he would serve a life sentence. In Germany, a life sentence means that a criminal must be in jail for fifteen years before being considered for parole, not necessarily that a criminal will serve the rest of his days behind bars.

The Bundesgerichtshof, or Federal Court of Justice, Germany's highest court in civil and criminal matters, would decide to accept or refuse any proposed appeal. The type of appeal applicable in Armin's case would be based on questions of the law only, and not on a renewed investigation into the facts of the case. If such an appeal took place, the sentence by the Kassel regional court would be rendered invalid.

Many legal experts were eager to see an appeal take place. According to Lorenz Böllinger, Bremer legal professor and psychologist, Armin should have been convicted of murder for sexual satisfaction in the first instance. "Our society can't accept that someone is killed to be eaten," he said. "I predict that the Federal Court will say that it simply won't do." Böllinger also claimed the Kassel regional court should have granted Armin Meiwes diminished responsibility so that he could be locked up in a psychiatrist clinic. "In my opinion, the man is urgently in need of treatment."

Maybe
It's Going
to Happen
Again

Armin was feeling more stable than he had in years.

In fact, he hadn't felt this balanced since living at home with his father and brothers as a little boy. The sense of community prison life offered him resembled the big family he had always longed for. He was constantly surrounded by people and thrived on the attention that he received, both from the inmates and psychiatrists inside jail, as well as from the fans and media outside the prison walls. And his daily routine gave him a series of minor goals he knew he could accomplish.

Naturally, he suffered from a certain sense of confinement; he was restricted in his movements and in his personal space. But ironically, he also experienced a great sense of freedom, at least within his head. Since the trial, he had been released from the mental torment that had plagued him every day and night of his adult life. The whirlwind of cannibalistic thoughts and impulses that regularly raged through his mind had quieted down to a steady hum. For once in his life, Armin had found a moderation of mental peace.

He now had the chance to share his thoughts about cannibalism; he spent many enjoyable sessions revealing them to prison psychiatrists. They strove to understand the troubled individual that he presented, while Armin obtained a tremendous sense of relief as he unburdened his internal anguish, his cannibalistic cravings and his imaginary world, without fear of judgment or rejection. He knew he could disclose all of his dark secrets safely to the doctors—they couldn't tell anyone else without first seeking his permission.

After the trial and the sentencing, Armin felt he had mastered his urge to eat someone, at least to a certain extent. It was still an integral part of him, a need that nagged him, but he felt he was able to keep it in check. As far as he was concerned, he had satisfied his desire to incorporate a "younger brother" as a part of himself, and that desire was not going to recur. Therefore, he could master his cannibalistic tendencies. True, he savored the memory of his first bite of human meat, and knew he would never lose his appetite for human flesh now that he had tasted it. But he also knew that within the prison walls, he would behave himself and eat bland prison food: his typical menu now consisted of pasta, vegetables or meat, mostly pork. He realized that although he would never forget it, he was expected to put his cannibalistic life behind him, focus on his new life and prepare for his eventual release.

Medical experts didn't share Armin's optimism about the improved state of his mental health. Dr. Rudolf Egg, the criminal psychologist who had testified at Armin's trial, did not believe his mental health had improved while under surveillance and locked behind bars; rather, he believed Armin's cannibal urges simply lay dormant. He reasoned that the perversion had taken a long time to develop; it wasn't going to simply disappear over night. Egg also doubted that Armin was experiencing genuine regret for having killed and eaten Bernd. He acknowledged Armin no doubt regretted having been *found out*—but the way he had grinned in court when describing his crime was sufficient evidence to convince Egg that Armin hadn't developed any deep feelings of remorse for his actions. In Egg's opinion, Armin would represent a certain threat to society if he were to be let loose again.

Arthur Kreuzer, professor for criminology at Giessen University, also didn't believe Armin could completely tame his wild desires. "This is a severe perversion and will be with him for life," Kreuzer said. "It can't be treated. The only thing that can be done for someone like that is just to learn to live their life with it without acting out their perversion and avoiding certain situations."

Mark Benecke, a German forensic criminologist, as well cast doubt on Armin's alleged recovery and his ability to calm the beast within. "It's his way of having sex, or the way that he wants to have sex," Benecke said. "It's a kind of disorder. People like that can't control their urges; they can't even control thinking about it."

The professional community was worried that when released, Armin would cannibalize someone else.

Criminologists and psychologists also feared that Armin's relatively light sentence, his sudden rise to fame and the promise of riches might inspire other people to follow his cannibalistic example. "The borders aren't there anymore," Benecke said. "The subcultures are getting very well connected. Maybe it's going to happen again. Maybe not in our lifetime again in Germany, but you never know."

Armin's cannibalism was already being linked to a string of crimes committed in the aftermath of his trial, arousing a great deal of concern in Germany. The police in the German state of Lower Saxony suspected a connection between Armin's trial and an instance of high school violence. A group of teenagers in the city of Hildesheim tortured a fellow student—and videotaped their actions, which included forcing their victim to lick their shoes and to brush his teeth with household cleaner. The police believed videotaping the sessions was inspired by the filming of Bernd's slaughter, and that the teenagers had been attracted by the idea of money. "They thought, 'Maybe if we can make a film [of our crime], we can make some money too,'" said Christian Pfeiffer, a former state justice minister who is now director of the Criminology Institute of Lower Saxony.

Armin may also have influenced a crime in the U.K. In February 2004, horrified police officers found the dismembered body of a man after they were called to a flat in East London. Blood was splattered on the walls and floor, and the perpetrator was frying the victim's brain in the kitchen, in a pan on the stove. The body, believed to be that of Brian Cherry, the forty-five-year-old bachelor tenant of the flat, had suffered multiple injuries, including dismemberment. The suspect had been released hours earlier from a mental home.

Armin never learned about this other cannibal's crime. But he probably would have enjoyed the gory details. It also might have given him ideas.

For the future.